THE ACTRESS IN THE PUBLIC THEATRES OF CALCUTTA

The Actress in the Public Theatres of Calcutta

Sarvani Gooptu

PRIMUS BOOKS

PRIMUS BOOKS

An imprint of Ratna Sagar P. Ltd.
Virat Bhavan
Mukherjee Nagar Commercial Complex
Delhi 110 009

Offices at

CHENNAI LUCKNOW

AGRA AHMEDABAD BANGALORE COIMBATORE
DEHRADUN GUWAHATI HYDERABAD JAIPUR JALANDHAR
KANPUR KOCHI KOLKATA MADURAI MUMBAI
PATNA RANCHI VARANASI

First published 2015

ISBN: 978-93-84082-21-5

PUBLISHED BY PRIMUS BOOKS

Laser typeset by Guru Typograph Technology
Crossings Republic, Ghaziabad 201 009

Printed and bound in India by Replika Press Pvt. Ltd.

CONTENTS

ACKNOWLEDGEMENTS

THE IDEA OF working on the contribution and identity of the actress in the public theatres of Calcutta dawned on me when I was reading the theatre journals during my research on Dwijendralal Roy and the rise of nationalism in Bengal for my Ph.D. dissertation. The awareness of their contribution to the development of a new culture and a new mentality was nurtured by my stint as Research Officer at the Women's Studies Research Centre of the University of Calcutta. Professor Bharati Ray not only taught me to be sensitive to the role and contribution of women in all aspects of life, society and politics but also inculcated in me a sense of confidence in my own ability to pursue research work. I also greatly benefitted from my association there with Professor Mukul Mukherjee, Dr Nandini Bhattacharya Panda, Dr Paula Banerjee and Professor Krishna Sen.

However, it was much later when I completed my doctorate that I started work on this subject and I was greatly helped by a Minor Research Grant provided by the University Grants Commission (UGC) for a part of this work. I am indebted to the help extended to me by the Librarians and Staff of National Library, specially Ashim Mukhopadhyay who made sure that I got every book or journal I asked for, Bangiya Sahitya Parishad, Nehru Memorial Museum and Library, Aurobindo Bhavan Library and Natya Shodh Sansthan where I remember with gratitude the warm help provided to me by Pratibha Agarwal.

I am grateful to Dr Sipra Mukherjee, my friend of many years, and Dr Purna Chowdhury with whom I developed an instant rapport, for graciously responding to my request to translate some of the poems of the actresses. I have no hesitation in declaring that their work is so good that at times they seem better than the original.

During my research in Delhi, I was overwhelmed by the love, hospitality, and support I received from Dr R. Mahalakshmi and

Dr Rakesh Batabyal and their adorable children Krishna and Vishnu. I also received great help from all the staff members of the Academic Staff College. I must thank my lovely friends, Dr Visalakshi Menon, Professor Mridula Mukherjee, Professor Aditya Mukherjee and Professor Sucheta Mahajan and Dr Bodh Prakash with whom I had lively and fruitful discussions on actresses and many other subjects. I have learnt so much from my repeated interactions with them. I must acknowledge with gratitude the great support that Dr Susmita Dasgupta has given me whenever I have requested it and all the times that I have picked her brains on different aspects of my research. I thank my friends Udit and Sanjukta Mitra and Debashish Sur, with whom I have stayed whenever I have gone to Delhi.

Professor Gautam Bhadra set me on the path of research and over the years has patiently taught me to be passionate and meticulous about it, never taking the easy way out and has set a very high standard which I will always strive to achieve. Professor Sekhar Bandopadhyay has always mentored and inspired me whenever I have faltered. I am truly grateful to him. I also thank my teachers Professor Suranjan Das, Professor Arun Bandopadhyay, Professor Hari Vasudevan, Professor Bhaskar Chakraborty and my friends Dr Suparna Gooptu and Dr Sanjukta Dasgupta at the Department of History, University of Calcutta for always being there for me.

Professor Krishna Bose, Professor Sugata Bose and Dr Sumantra Bose have always treated me as part of their family and I am grateful for their constant love and encouragement. I gratefully acknowledge my friends and the staff at Netaji Bhavan with whom I spend so much time during seminars, meetings and programmes.

My colleagues and friends at the Calcutta Girls College are my greatest assets since they always inspire and encourage me through regular discussions and advice and I must specially acknowledge Dr Nandini Bhattacharya, Dr Ruma Bhattacharyya, Dr Nayeem Ahmed, Dr Yasmin Akhtar, Supritha Mukhopadhyay, Sanchita Dey and Chandranath Saha. I must thank my long-time friends Dr Susmita Mukherjee, Dr Ishita Banerjee Dube, Gargi Gangopadhyay, Arpita Mukherjee, Ruplekha Sur (whom I lost some years back), Sayantani and Avishek Dutt, Nandita and Aditya Palchaudhuri, Arun and Anupama Jhunjhunwala, Chanda Dutt and Raka Sen for allowing me to whine and grumble about my life and work at all times.

I must thank Dr Lipi Ghosh, Dr Suchandra Ghosh, Dr Sarita Khettri, Dr Rajasree Basu and all my colleagues and friends at the

Indian Association of Asian and Pacific Studies for providing me with a forum to present my research at the seminars held there. I must also thank Dr Lipi Ghosh for introducing me to the pleasure of teaching postgraduate students of Gender Studies at the Department of South and South-East Asian Studies. I would also like to thank Natya Shodh Sansthan, Kolkata for the photographs.

I must thank my parents Nirendra Nath and Bijaya Dutta, my parents-in-law Ajit and Arundhati Gooptu, my siblings Indrani and Indranath Bose, Sakti and Brian Kunz, Dr Suvendranath and Rajakumari D. Dutta, Adheep and Sohini Gooptu and the adorable next generation Dr Aniruddha and Frances Bose, Ahon and Abon Gooptu, Arunendro and Rajendro Dutta for their enduring love and support.

Last but not the least, I could not have done anything in life without the help, criticism and constant support of my husband Pradeep Gooptu and the encouragement, technical and emotional, of my children, Subhalakshmi and Siddhesh Gooptu.

I extend my gratitude to all of you.

Kolkata SARVANI GOOPTU

INTRODUCTION

THEATRE HAS BEEN in the blood of the Bengalis ever since rudimentary beginnings were made by the Russian traveller Gerasim Lebedeff in 1795. In the theatrical performance organized by Lebedeff at Domtolla in north Calcutta, women performed in the female roles. But the theatre he established could not continue for long and there followed a lull of some years till Nabin Chandra Basu organized the production of the popular play *Bidyasundar* in 1835 with both men and women performers. Though it was a resounding success, this venture too could not continue beyond a few performances. Its critics were too many and too loud and its resources at hand too little. It was obvious that theatre for the Bengalis in Calcutta had not yet come of age.

During this period, English theatre was very popular in various halls in Calcutta and this kept the dream that Lebedeff started and Nabin Chandra embellished, alive in the hearts of theatre-lovers of the city. Bengali theatrical tradition survived in the Jatras, innovated to suit the new sophisticated taste of the Bengali *Bhadralok* and in the private theatres in the houses of the rich and powerful of Calcutta and the suburbs. The performances that followed were before a restricted audience and the performances were entirely by men from a middle-class background. It was only in 1872 that thc doors were open to the public with paying the price of a ticket being the only restriction for entry to the hall of magic. Theatre sponsored in the houses of the rich Bengalis had already become the benchmark of wealth and culture. Yet till 1872, it remained out of reach of the rest of society though Western education and Western contact and consequently money was filtering into the middle ranks of the society. So when it opened to the public, theatre-going became the symbol of social mobility as well as the means of showing off one's wealth and culture.[1] Magical it certainly was with women acting in female roles once again after five decades on 16 August 1873, in Bengal Theatre in Michael Madhusudan Dutta's *Sarmishtha* with Jagattarini, Golaap, Elokeshi and Shyama. The next year, August 1874, saw Great National Theatre introducing actresses Kadambini, Kshetramoni, Jadumoni, Haridashi and Rajkumari in *Sati Ki Kalankini*.

This work is mainly a study of the participation of women in the theatre of Bengal, when actresses started performing regularly on stage in the public theatres instead of young boys in women's roles. Although many books have been written on the theatre of Bengal, very few have concentrated on the actresses and their contribution to the profession or to their position in society or their ideas about art and themselves as gleaned from available contemporary sources.

A word of explanation as to why I use 'actress' instead of the more politically correct term 'actor' to denote performers in a drama no matter which sex they belong to. First of all, this connotation is relatively a recent one and does not apply to the period I have portrayed here. More importantly I have tried to trace how women entered into the male bastion of acting and how they fought hard to establish their position there during the first six decades of public theatre. This fight was to first obtain a foothold and then to stand upright in a crowd of actors who constantly pushed the actresses back, hand-in-glove with the critics and analysts of the performances. It would take many more decades for the actress to fight for gender equality. I have ended the story in the 1930s when the idea of theatre only as entertainment was gradually questioned and drama involved the portrayal of contemporary ideas and concepts as well as had a political agenda similar to that which was present in the first half of the twentieth century, and yet was different. More importantly, the role of the actress changed and performers were subsumed by the content of the plays and its agenda. The focus shifted from the performers to the ideas and ideology.

With the beginning of colonial rule, the need of the colonizers to acquaint themselves with the colonized country brought a new Orientalist mission as executed through the Asiatic Society. A monumental project of translations of Sanskrit texts were begun and with it came the discovery of India's past and its interpretation. The study of Indian drama and writing on it was the effort of the Asiatic Society and other Indologists after the publication of Sir William Jones' translation of Kalidasa's *Abhjnana Shakuntalam* in 1789.

This was followed by a number of Sanskrit plays being translated[2] and a number of scholarly works on Indian theatre by Indologists under the aegis of the Asiatic Society. Among the many works in this genre I have taken up four texts of H.H. Wilson (1827), Sylvain Levi (1890), E.P. Horrwitz (1912) and Keith (1924) and tried to find the sources of the historiography of drama. These scholars were translating and examining Sanskrit texts (drama included) not only as part of the syllabus of oriental studies for their officials but also to present to their readers in Western Societies a new archive of literary work of high standards from a time when Western Societies were not that mature. It was possibly also a part of the representation of the exotic Orient as the repository of the highest culture. These translations provided the opportunity for performances in Calcutta immediately as reports in the Calcutta Gazette show. Jones' translation of *Abhigyan Shakuntalam* was followed by appreciation as a 'pleasing and authentic picture of old Hindu manners', to be performed as a successful play by 'insolvent debtors (theatre owners)'.[3] It is also my postulate that they were writing at a time when theatre was running to full houses in Calcutta and which these writers were aware of. (English theatre in the case of Wilson in 1827, and Bengali theatre as well for Horrwitz, Keith, Schroeder, Pischel, Hertel, Ridgeway, Luders and Konow in the 1920s.) There were also debates and analyses of the drama being presented in the English language newspapers of the day which may have inspired a desire to find the sources of present issues. It cannot be possible that their interest was not influenced by that though they all tried to stay loyal to their patron body, the Asiatic Society, by following more or less the same forms and format though nuances in content changed over the next hundred years.

Horace H. Wilson in 1827 dedicated the *Select Specimens of the Theatre of the Hindus* to His Most Gracious Majesty George the Fourth as the patron of Oriental Literature in order that he may 'familiarize his British Subjects with the manners and feelings of their fellow subjects on the East'[4] specially since as he stressed that 'Europe possessed no dramatic literature before fourteenth–fifteenth century at which period the Hindu drama had passed into oblivion'.[5] He also wrote in the introduction that 'his ambition' in translating the six Sanskrit dramas and comments on twenty-three Sanskrit plays was, 'to secure to the Hindu theatre a place in English Literature. It was not', he avowed, his purpose, 'to furnish the student of Sanskrit with a class book'. This, of course, was not a negation of his association with the Orientalist project but more an explanation that his translation was not a literal one. In fact, when the original texts were published by the Committee of Public Instruction, he compared them and made alterations in his second edition.[6] E.P. Horrwitz in *The Indian Theatre* (1912) too endeavours 'to touch the very soul of the old Sanskrit plays'.[7] He, besides being a Lecturer in Sanskrit in Trinity College, was an Assistant Examiner to the Civil Service Commission.[8] His work, like that of Levi, paid attention to antiquity, tracing the beginning of Indian drama to the beginning of history in India.[9] As and when various texts on drama were being translated, these projects on their analysis were also undertaken. Just like Wilson, Sylvain Levi (1890) was inspired to write on Indian theatre when William Jones' translation appeared in different European languages from the 1780s to the 1880s. His *Le Theatre Indien* in two volumes in the 1890s had a great impact on later research as has been testified to by later writers. Even Rabindranath Tagore invited Levi to Santiniketan for the inauguration of Visva-Bharati. Montgomery Schuler in 1906 published a *Bibliography of the Sanskrit Drama* and A. Berriedale Keith's *The Sanskrit Drama in its Origin: Development, Theory and Practice*[10] was published in 1924.

If these works are taken as a whole, despite the difference in the time of writing, certain observations may be made on the basis of their original purpose. Along with tracing the history of drama in different periods, there is also detailed discussion in these works on the origin of Indian drama. Following the established norms in trying to establish a lineage, a comparative analysis is made with Greek drama. Though the writers followed the established practice, there was no consensus among them and they were aware that there was a possibility that indigenous developments may have had the greatest influence. That is why folk culture and indigenous drama forms are also studied. Wilson has also compared it with Chinese drama.[11] He also wrote that a 'perusal of the Hindu plays will present characteristic varieties of conduct and construction which strongly evidence both original design and national development.'[12] It is obvious from the writing of Keith that in the Asiatic Society project which was undertaken after the publishing of the translations of Bhasa and Asvaghosa, a debate ensued among the seven researches regarding the origin of the Sanskrit dramas. Most of them however followed Wilson, Levi and Horrwitz to negate the influence on various grounds.[13] Horrwitz compares every drama he discusses with a close parallel in Western or English drama or literature so that his readers connect with what he is discussing at once.[14] The other point to note is that all the works discuss dramatic practices in detail in more or less a similar routine—dramatic arrangement, plot, characters, objects of dramatic representation, diction and scenic representation (Wilson), treatises in dramaturgy, dramatic art, dramatic aesthetics, dramatic practice (Sylvain Levi), and dramatic theory, treatises in dramatic art, nature and types of drama, plot, characters sentiments, styles, language and music (Keith).

There is another notable point—all the works discussed the other indigenous influences as well and all of them show a close awareness of the various art forms. This I believe could not have been possible unless they had first-hand knowledge of the various art forms present at the time they were writing. For example, Wilson in 1827 speaks of forms 'of an inferior description and which existed sometimes apparently in the vernacular dialects . . .'. He is referring to the Bhanas in the Jatras of Bengal.[15] Horrwitz discusses Bhanas (musical sketches of south India)[16] and the Jatras of Bengal whose origin he traces from the Vedic period[17] and ends with Keshav Chandra Sen writes, 'made use of the stage to popularize his religious views'.[18] Keith disagrees with Sylvain Levi that Sanskrit drama sprang first into being in Prakrit while Sanskrit was later applied when Sanskrit, long reserved as a sacred language, re-entered into use as the language of literature. Keith believes that it was only when 'Brahmin genius fused the ethnic and religious agnostic motives in to a new creation of the highest importance . . .' the drama was created.[19] Others like Hildebrandt and Weber connect it to popular mime and epics[20] and Pischel (1902) to puppet play, etc.

The final point which I would like to stress in these Orientalist writings is that they all discuss 'national' in theatre. In their writings, the sensibilities and experiences of the writers themselves play a part. The idea of culture playing an important role in nationalism was already an important discussion in the second half of the nineteenth century. Horrwitz in 1912 speaks of how Sanskrit drama became national as the *Ramayana* and *Mahabharata* spread all over the country through various interpretations and in Ceylon as well.[21] They are aware that national for Sanskrit plays could only have been a horizontal spread over a certain educated elite section. In fact, Wilson signified this when he wrote that the peculiarity of the dramas was that since Sanskrit is no longer spoken, though the compositions are 'relatively modern, they must, therefore, be unintelligible to a considerable proportion of their audiences and never could have been so directly addressed to the bulk of the population', unlike the performances of 'an inferior description' which '... numerous, popular and were strictly speaking national.'[22] Though it is not present in the writings of Wilson, Horrwitz or Keith, in Levi's work there is a chapter on modern and contemporary theatre where he discusses 'yatras', 'revival of classical dramas after 1857', 'western influence' through the performance of 'British actors in the big cities', 'contemporary theatre in Aryan India' by which he means the Bengali plays, some of which he discusses as well. He has also discussed theatre production in Gujarati, Punjabi, Tamil and the Parsi theatre.[23] Levi concludes that the Indian theatre is representative of the inconsistency and strangeness that India is—an amalgam of ancient conventions and customs coexisting with innovations without losing vitality and originality. He believes that the new circumstances (possibly meaning colonial rule) have brought a new impetus to theatre after a period of lethargy. Yet Western influence has not created the new theatre. In his words, 'Western influence is a negligible quantity. It catches the eye because it is superficial. Indian modern theatre is a worthy heir of the ancient'.[24] No wonder that Levi was such an inspiration to later generations of cultural nationalists.

These researches into the Indian literary past and the sense of pride that it generated could not have left educated Indians immune and this sense of pride manifested itself in nationalism. The idea which may have come to the minds of the Western-educated in India and abroad, was that even the research into India's cultural past could be done by the Indians themselves. The proliferation of texts and writings in journals on the past is proof of this. That I am separating this genre from the motivated nationalist writing is because though the need to arouse patriotism had been at the back of Indian minds since the mid-nineteenth century, these writings are less inspirational and more investigative in the research on theatre of the present through the light of the past. In the case of Bengal, most of the writings in the journals are in Bengali and there are analytical writings on Western theatre and music as well as discussions on the comparative value of Eastern and Western culture.

Theatre was discussed as an art form by those passionately involved in theatre as actors and managers, as well as by those who influenced by the work of the Orientalists and wanted to bring Bengali theatre into the focus of the world. They not only discuss the content of the plays, the important characters, but created classification formats of mythological, religious, patriotic, social, farces, which are still followed today. A number of books on the history of Bengali drama and theatre were also written over the ages in Bengali starting with *Bangiya Natyashalar Itihas* by Brojendranath Bandopadhyay.[25] Two important texts, which became path-breaking models for later authors, were written in English by Prabhu Charan Guha Thakurta[26] (*The Bengali Drama: Its Origin and Development* in 1930) and Hemendranath Dasgupta (*The Indian Theatre*). They were both Doctoral theses awarded by London University but straddled both worlds of describing the content as well as the form of the dramas performed on the Bengal stage. Both these books however aimed to bring into the focus of the world, the developments in theatre in Bengal and the origin of the dramatic form. The style followed more or less that of the Orientalists, only the content was more detailed and definitive. In fact, Hemendranath Dasgupta even had the General Secretary, Johan Van Manen of the Asiatic Society, writing his preface. Similar writing may be seen in the work of R.K. Yagnik who published *The Indian Theatre: Its Origin and its Later Development under European Influence* in 1933 where he describes the theatre in western India. Hemendranath Dasgupta considers the Bengal stage as playing an important role in the making of modern Bengal, since the study of the stage is vital to 'fully comprehend the bend of national genius'.[27] He started working on the book from 1915 using modern techniques or research. He quoted copiously from newspapers and journals and established their authenticity in the study of the theatre, both English and Bengali.[28] He traced the history of the theatre from the time of the *Rig Veda* down to the English theatre in Calcutta and the start of the theatre in Bengali in the first volume. What was different in his writing is that he devoted a section to actresses who were introduced into English theatre in Calcutta in 1788.[29] Hemendranath showed that even in English theatre, debates ensued when plans started to introduce actresses. He referred to the article of Mrs Fay in Hartley House where she lauds the absence of actresses in Calcutta and upholds that the example should be followed in England where playhouses have become 'nurseries of vice and public seraglios far more censurable and licentious than any Eastern world contains . . .'.[30] Finally, despite all misgivings 'a numerous assembly was attracted by the novel appearance of a lady whose condescension to grace the Calcutta Stage would alone entitle her to lasting remembrance . . .' (on 18 December 1788, as reported by the *Calcutta Gazette*).[31] Kironmoy Raha in 1978 also did a detailed survey of theatre in Calcutta as well as Jatra and English theatre.[32]

There are many works in Bengali on theatre and drama, their content and performances in the early phase of the public theatre[33] as well as innumerable writings in the leading journals of the time and later.[34] Yet in all these works there are only fragmented references to the actresses. Even in the recent works of modern scholars[35] of drama and theatre where minute research initiative with analytical ability has been combined, few of them which deal with the actress, and none in entirety. The only definitive work was a translation of the autobiography of Binodini Dasi by Rimli Bhattacharya (1998) where in the Introduction to the work and Notes on Bengali Public Theatre, she described the world of the actress in detail as well as in the Afterword, describes the evolution of Binodini into an iconic figure.[36] My inspiration to look into the world of the actress came from reading Binodini Dasi's autobiography republished in 1987[37] as well as numerous references and analyses of the contribution of the actress as an artist and her impact on contemporary society in contemporary journals in Bengali and English.

Any writing on women needs to be placed within the scholarship of feminism in cultural studies which has engaged the mind of writers on theatre in all countries. The very fact that replacing male actors in female roles by women had to be introduced in the midst of vociferous protests was in itself a political statement on gender. Sustaining their new occupation in the face of social disapproval, fighting their own insecurities and establishing a new identity was more a question of survival for the women than a sense of sexual freedom which Richard Findlater writing on actresses in Stuart England talks about when he claims that the actresses achieved sexual freedom and limited women's liberation.[38] Nandi Bhatia's recent study, *Performing Women, Performing Womanhood* (2010)[39] is one of the very few books devoted solely to the gender issue in theatre in detail. She has focused on women who perform on the borderlines of theatre and write on or perform in dramas that contest middle-class codes through dramatic enactments which developed in the national popular consciousness. She also placed some dramas in the backdrop of the social reform movements, major political developments and post-colonial issues and discussed social dissensions regarding caste and gender. Rimli Bhattacharya, in 1998, by editing and translating the autobiography of Binodini Dasi, one of the pioneers of Bengali theatre, has brought to the notice of the non-Bengali reader, the contradictions in the life of an actress as well as one of the first 'non-*Bhadramahila* writing'. Binodini was probably not the first public woman to write her memoirs since Nabin Kali Debi's *Kamini Kalanka*[40] had already been published long before in 1870 and many women were publishing autobiographical or fictional writing in Bengali journals. But her autobiography was very important since it still remains the only available writing by an actress of that era. In the Introduction to the translation of *My Story and My Life as an Actress*, Bhattacharya has explored through the autobiography the 'mutually informing role ambiguous construction of her sexuality in performance and in the perception of the actress as a sex object and most importantly reworking of traditional material in the person and body of the actress'.[41] In my work, I have brought in many more angles concerning the management, experiences of other actresses, as well as the society which loomed large before the actress, which she wanted to be a part of and negotiated in various ways to achieve that objective. On the other hand, there were the society leaders who could within a decade no longer ignore the presence of the actress and tried to portray them as outcasts, yet not completely outside the social boundaries. Minoti Chatterjee in her book *Theatre Beyond the Threshold* discusses how from 1905, the cultural protest movement, 'sought to challenge the values of the dominant culture and to create alternatives'.[42] In a few paragraphs in the Introduction she also brings in issues of feminism within the theatre. She talks about the paradoxes arising from the troubled question of female sexuality which emerged with the entry of the actress in theatre along with the very strength of lack of family bindings which made her perfect for public life and which in itself condemned her as a public woman with no morals.[43] Ananda Lal argues that though actresses were inducted in the late nineteenth century, it was considered as not really affecting middle class morality since the actresses did not come from 'respectable' families. But Rabindranath Tagore broke major social barriers when he brought in women of his family in performances in Jorasanko, as well as explored female sexuality in *Chitrangada* and wrote *Natir Puja* with only female characters. Even in other parts of the country, acceptability of women on stage was a major step in the progress of modernization.[44] Malini

Bhattacharya's survey of the dramatic performances in the Indian People's Theatre Association movement[45] in the districts surprisingly does not touch upon the tensions of gender relations which must have existed within the theatre groups. Neera Adarkar, brings in interesting insights into the role, participation and position of women in Marathi theatre (1843–1933) not only in acting in male and female roles but also establishing and running theatrical companies.[46]

Recent studies are taking the threshold of theatre studies beyond the colonial period and Anuradha Kapur through her study of women theatre practitioners in Hindi show how their work has shifted the debate towards new forms and new subjectivities by using new strategies, to study experiences that have been invisible till now.[47]

The questions on the identity of the actress were raised almost at the same time as the question of morality and a constant parallel was drawn between the actresses of the West and in Bengal. All the journals which discussed theatre in later nineteenth and early twentieth-century Bengal focused on the position and contribution of actresses in Western countries. In the biographies being written by men at the time the actress was, in most cases, being brought into discussion, but these two issues need to be studied in detail.

In *The Actress in the Public Theatres of Calcutta*, I have started the story a little before 1873 which was the date when five women from the 'forbidden areas' (*nishidhhapalli*) performed in women's roles in public theatre. What I find interesting is that there was always a *presence* of actresses throughout the period from 1795 to 1873, even when they were absent in reality. Actresses appear constantly in the minds of the audience and the critics. So the contribution of the actress has to be seen against the backdrop of the entire history of the Bengali stage—why the use of actresses was discontinued, after brief experiments in 1795 and 1835, why there were no actresses in the amateur theatres, not even from respectable families, despite the fact that the new style jatras used women in female roles during the same period. But there was a consciousness of the need in the minds of those associated with theatre which finally manifested in the new style public theatre started in 1872 initially in Bengal theatre and then others as well. The whole process naturally generated tremendous discussion which I have brought in from contemporary evidence.

A storm accompanied the entry of the actress through both accolades and stern criticism. The fact that the only women available for the stage were from the prostitute quarters stirred the sensibilities of 'respectable' society. Other than rudimentary artistic training, not much was expected from these women, and yet the returns were brilliant. The second chapter sketches this picture of the actress who was brought to the stage reluctantly, was considered a necessary evil, yet who managed ably to fulfil the role assigned to her. It also traces the tensions and contradictions in the career and life of actresses who never really got their due. The actress remained a good student, a brilliant performer yet was never able to overtake the 'lead' actor in the choice of roles, monetary matters or in fame. She was also subordinated by her 'loyalty' to her mentor or patron and this loyalty in her career and personal life often hindered her ambition. The position of the actress always remained subordinate in this early period of the professional theatre (1872–1920) called actors' theatre by many critics in contrast to the producers' theatre of the post-1920s.

Initially there was very little expectation of good performance from the actresses since it was known that they were from backward and uneducated sections. But when night after night in different plays, they performed brilliantly, the praise of the critics became unstinted. How could these prostitutes transform into characters of 'noble women' or 'heavenly goddesses'? Though they were uneducated, they were able to interpret the complexities of human nature and even portray Anglicized Bengali characters with English-based dialogues. With aplomb they acted in historical tragedies portraying strong and complicated characters. This training process I have discussed in my second chapter.

All the leading dramatists of the time appreciated the performance of these women who despite their disadvantages could present such sterling interpretations of the greatest works of the time. Bengali theatre came of age when the Bengali men of literature wrote drama which was brilliantly adapted to the public stage and it was no longer necessary to dramatize great literature. Some of these plays were written specifically for the stage while others had a reading public in mind but were adapted for the public theatre by the actors and directors. In all of them, the actresses put in sterling performances and often worked night and day to perfect difficult characterizations. In the third chapter, I have dealt with some performances by leading actresses for dramas written by two stalwart Bengali dramatists—Dwijendralal Roy and Rabindranath Tagore, who were not directly associated with the theatre, but whose plays became exemplary pieces for performance at all times.

It is said that beauty lies in the eyes of the beholder. For the visual and performing arts this is undeniably true. No matter how well a play is written, its success is ultimately judged by the response of the audience. The relationship between drama and the audience has since time immemorial been interactive. However, with the establishment of private and professional theatres, there was the beginning of a separation between the fictional stage world and the audience. Admission prices limited the social composition of the audience and with it came the beginning of passivity of audience and the emergence of a code and conventions of behaviour. The theatre design of stalls replacing pits ensured sedate behaviour and footlights became the literal barrier which separated the audience from the stage. But the involvement of the audience both during and outside the performance remained constant. Their influence was present in pre-production—writing of the drama, casting, advertisement, during production—acting styles, introduction of music and dance and post-production in the critical appraisal of the viewers. Economically, the theatre is tied to the willing audience who pays to watch the performance and the sponsors and patrons of theatre. Any new directions in the shape of both new playwriting and new performance objectives/techniques depend on the audience' taste which is notoriously fickle. Also compared to other public media, this tie with the audience is more in theatre since it faces a live audience and the response is immediate, be it applause or brickbats. Again, how long a play runs also depends on the whims of the audience. In fact, the success or failure of a dramatic performance depends less on its content and quality and more on its acceptance by the audience. It is also undeniable that through all the vicissitudes of the fortunes and the allure of other entertainment in twentieth-century Calcutta, the theatre survived largely due to the loyalty of its audience. It is no mean credit that ultimately no one in the city, from the school going teenager and the demure, pious housewife to the spiritual leader of the age, Sri Ramkrishna Paramhansa, was immune to the magic of the stage.

It is however also a very difficult arena to map because the audience does not normally leave any systematic and continuous record of its reaction. When the study is of theatre in the past, the task is not only difficult but daunting. A researcher has to depend only on newspaper or journal reports and the memory of all the people concerned.

Sometimes, its reflection is seen in contemporary literature. It is from all these sources that I have tried to, in the fourth chapter, visualize the audience of early twentieth-century Calcutta—the public who visited the professional theatres at a time when the theatre wove its magic over the society, when theatre had to be hated or loved but never ignored and before cinema cast its mesmerizing bait.

A debate which became vital in the second decade of the twentieth century forms the basis of my fifth chapter—whether there was a conflict between box office success and the integrity of art. After all, a change had occurred over a century of theatrical productions—from the amateur theatres by moneyed men who had the means and space to indulge in their passion to theatre post-1870s which became serious ventures since they were neither free productions nor performed for an invited audience. Theatre had a dual responsibility to those who paid for its production as well as those who paid to watch it. Thus, public theatre was a serious business proposition. The love for the art remained with those connected with theatre but survival and competition became a serious issue. Of course the actress was always intimately connected with every twist and turn of fortune since theatre could no longer be envisaged without the actress. Patronage of theatre still remained with the aristocratic Bengalis who believed that love for the art could triumph over the stigma that theatre faced from the 1870s with it becoming an arena of clandestine pleasure for the rich which sometimes led to ruin of many families. But a new dimension also entered when a new form of patronage entered the arena with certain business groups looking at theatre purely from the point of view of a profitable business venture. All these new developments brought up many issues of conflict among different theatres and a new spirit of professionalism came of age. In a way it also brought about an air of liberation for the actress. The stranglehold of the mentor/director/patron was inevitably loosened in these anarchical conditions. In the fifth chapter, I discuss how the actress saw the clash of the titans between the old-style production of Girish Ghosh and the new-style production of Amarendranath Datta. It was not simply the establishment of a new theatre but a challenge of the traditional order which was considered sacrilegious by most yet must have been admired, albeit secretly, as well.

A sense of liberation was inevitable. Not that anyone could dream of an open rebellion against a mentor or a patron, but there are many paths to survival. One of them was of course the courts. It was

Amarendranath who indirectly started this and the process he started boomeranged against him. Many more actresses continued to seek the shelter of the court in the process started by Tarasundari and some actually won their legal battles. Unfortunately, it was also a means which the theatres used to keep the actress tied down to their contracts. This is a fascinating world of litigation where the revelations and verdicts are no less dramatic than the dramas themselves. I explore a few cases in the sixth chapter where some of the leading actresses were involved in order to see whether it was a sense of empowerment or survival that motivated the actresses.

How much was the actress of Bengali theatre in the late nineteenth–early twentieth century aware of her artistic identity? Was she torn between the age-old fear of lack of future security and a desire for career satisfaction? Unlike in England, where the actress despite becoming the mistress of leading men of the court or even the royal family, continued to shine in her profession, in Bengal, shelter by a rich patron invariably included a demand to quit the theatre and it was complied to by her without any apparent hesitation. There are instances in England of married actors and actresses or even siblings performing on stage but that was unthinkable here. The stigma attached to acting was so severe and the longing for respectability and social acceptance so ingrained in the middle-class mentality of the age that the two were incompatible. Goshtho Behari married Golaap on the insistence of his mentor Upendranath Das who thought that was the path of social emancipation for a prostitute, but could not tolerate the taunts of society for having married an actress, notwithstanding the fact that Golaap a la the famed Sukumari had renounced acting at the height of her career. Such a great actress as Binodini Dasi, in recognition of whose acting talent a theatre was built, succumbed to the lure of financial security and retired to play the role of a domesticated mistress and remained in seclusion, at the age of only twenty-four though she was at the pinnacle of her career. And they were not petty actresses in side roles. They were the most talked—about women for decades to come. Yet they seemed to only want to replace their lost 'families' with, if not a legitimate one in the eyes of society, then at least one with some financial security. Is this the identity that a performing artist par excellence actually looks for? This is the question I have raised in the last chapter of the book. Besides biographical sketches of actresses of the time I have, in the Appendix, added a slice of writing of three of the best actresses on Bengali stage Binodini, Sukumari and Tarasundari in translation for a taste of their literary work.

What then was the view of actresses in contemporary eyes? Were they viewed only as destroyers of the morality of respectable men or were their talents appreciated? They faced tremendous difficulties, overcame great odds on the way to stardom. The actresses always acknowledged the contribution of their mentors and all those who helped them. The realization that the theatre brought not only professional satisfaction but also freedom from the stigma of their past life made these young girls work very hard to achieve the dream of recreating on stage lives and characters so different from their own. Only through great performances could they hope to make society forget that they were 'fallen' women who were destroying the lives of the respectable men who joined theatres unable to resist the passion which had been ignited in Bengal by an unknown Russian traveller. Sometimes, they ran away from this dream trying to chase another dream of a respectable family and security, but more often they wanted to see respect in the eyes of their audience and forget the pain of rejection by respectable society.

Notes

1, Abinash Chandra Gangopadhyay, *Girish Chandra: Banga Natyashalar Itihas Sambalito*, 1st pub. 1927, Calcutta: Dey's Publishing, 1977, p. 1.
2. Horace W. Wilson gives a list of 60 Hindu plays in 1827 in *Select Specimens of the Theatre of the Hindus*, 3 vols., 3rd edn., New Delhi: Asian Educational Services, 1984.
3. Quoted in Hemendranath Dasgupta, *The Indian Theatre*, vol. I, Delhi: Gyan Publishing House, 1988, p. 200.
4. Dedication in the 1stt edn., 16 May 1827, reprinted in Horace H. Wilson, 3rd edn., op. cit.
5. Ibid., Preface, p. xi.
6. Second edn., 15 December 1834, Oxford Advertisement, reprinted in Horace H. Wilson, 3rd edn., op. cit.
7. E.P. Horrwitz, *The Indian Theatre: A Brief Survey of the Sanskrit Drama*, London: Blackie and Son Ltd,. 1912, preface.
8. Ibid.
9. Ibid., two sections dealing with theatre during the Vedas to the Guptas, Sylvain Levi, Le Theatre Indien, 1890, *The Indian Theatre,* tr. Narayan Mukherjee, Calcutta: Writers Workshop, 1978, vol. II, pp. 1–52.

10. A.B. Keith, *The Sanskrit Drama in its Origin: Development, Theory and Practice*, Oxford: Clarendon Press, 1924, preface.
11. Wilson, op. cit., preface, p. xii.
12. Ibid., preface, p. xi.
13. Horrwitz, op. cit., pp. 76–7; Wilson, op. cit., preface, p. xi; Levi, op. cit., vol. II, pp. 53–73; Keith, op. cit.
14. He even compares Indian puppettry with Punch and Judy shows or dumbshows as he calls them. Horrwitz, op. cit., p. 159.
15. Wilson, op. cit., preface, p. xv.
16. Horrwitz, op. cit., pp. 174–5.
17. Ibid., p. 178 fn.
18. Ibid., p. 191.
19. Keith, op. cit., p. 46.
20. Discussed in detail in Keith, op. cit., pp. 46–56.
21. Wilson, op. cit., p. 77.
22. Wilson, op. cit., preface, p. xv.
23. Sylvain Levi, op. cit., pp. 97–119.
24. Ibid., pp. 118–19.
25. Brojendranath Bandopadhyay, *Bangiya Natyashala Itihas, 1795–1876*, Calcutta: Bangiya Sahitya Parishad, 5th edn., 1979,
26. Prabhu Charan GuhaThakurta, *The Bengali Drama: Its Origin and Development*, London: K. Paul, Trnch, Truber Pub., 1930.
27. Hemendranath Dasgupta, op. cit., Introductory chapter, p. i.
28. Ibid., p. 7.
29. Ibid., pp. 198–200.
30. Quoted in Hemendranath Dasgupta, op. cit., pp. 90–1.
31. Ibid.
32. Kironmoy Raha, *Bengali Theatre*, New Delhi: National Book Trust, 2001 (3rd edn.), first edn., 1978.
33. See Bibliography.
34. Advance, *Amrita Bazar Patrika* in English and *Nach Ghar, Natyamandir, Rangamancha, Rangalaya, Saurabh, Sisir*, etc., in Bengali.
35. For a study on historiography see Rakesh Soloman, 'Towards a Geneology of Indian Theatre Historiography and Ananda Lal: A Historiography of Modern Indian Theatre', in *Modern Indian Theatre: A Reader*, Nandi Bhatia, ed., Oxford University Press, 2009, pp. 1–40.
36. Rimli Bhattacharya, ed. and tr., Binodini Dasi, *My Story* and *My Life as an Actress*, New Delhi: Kali For Women, 1998.
37. Binodini Dasi, *Amar Kotha O Onyanyo Rochona*, ed. Soumitro Chattopadhyay and Nirmalya Acharya, Calcutta: Subarnarekha, repr. 1987.
38. Richard Findlater, *The Player Queens*, London: Weidenfeld and Nicolson, 1976.
39. Nandi Bhatia, *Performing Women/Performing Womanhood: Theatre, Politics and Dissent in North India*, New Delhi: Oxford University Press, 2010.

40. Nabin Kali Debi, *Kamini Kalanka*, 1277 BS, ed. Sumanta Banerjee, Kolkata: Wild Strawberries Books, 2010.
41. Rimli Bhattacharya, ed. and tr., Binodini Dasi, *My Story and My Life as an Actress*, New Delhi: Kali for Women, 1998, p. 12.
42. Minoti Chatterjee, *Theatre Beyond the Threshold: Colonialism, Nationalism and the Colonial State*, New Delhi: Indialog Publications Pvt. Ltd., 2004, p. 7.
43. Ibid., pp. 24–7.
44. Ananda Lal, 'A Historiography of Modern Indian Theatre', in *Modern Indian Theatre*, Nandi Bhatia, ed., op. cit., pp. 35–6.
45. Malini Bhattacharya, 'The Indian People's Theatre Associations: A Preliminary Sketch of the Movement and Organisation 1942–7', in *Modern Indian Theatre*, Nandi Bhatia, ed., op. cit., pp. 158–81.
46. Neera Adarkar, 'In Search of Women in History of Marathi Theatre', in *Modern Indian Theatre*, Nandi Bhatia, ed., pp. 219–32.
47. Anuradha Kapur, 'Reassembling the Modern: An Indian Theatre Map since Independence', in *Modern Indian Theatre*, Nandi Bhatia, ed., p. 49.

1

THE ENTRY OF THE ACTRESS IN PUBLIC THEATRE

THE HISTORY OF actresses in the public theatre of Calcutta has three watershed events. All three were concerned with public theatre and women in female roles. The first two events were isolated episodes but cast unforgettable shadows.

The first was the evening of 27 November 1795 when the curtain rose on the first Bengali play in the Bengally Theatre established by Gerasim Lebedeff, a Russian traveller in Calcutta, where actresses accompanied men. The performance was a Bengali translation of an English play, *The Disguise*, called 'Kalponik Sanbadal', translated by Lebedeff himself. The Bengali actors and actresses were brought in with the help of his 'Linguist Golok Nat Dash' which pleased him 'exceedingly'.[1] That was the beginning of Bengali theatre but one which ended after possibly only two performances. It would have seemed to be a mirage had it not been for another incident 39 years later.

On 6 October 1835, *Bidyasundar* was performed at the Shyambazar Theatre under the aegis of Nabin Chandra Basu. In this play at least three actresses again from the prostitute areas; Radhamoni, Joy Durga and Rajkumari, won instant acclaim. This theatre too did not last for long and was followed by a longer gap of 56 years.

The final event was on 16 August 1873, when in Bengal Theatre, which started as a public theatre the previous year selling tickets to anyone irrespective of background and class or caste, five actresses were brought in again from the prostitute quarters to act in Bengali plays. This was soon followed by other Bengali theatres as well. This time the practice proved to be permanent since neither theatre for public nor women acting in them has stopped ever since.

There are two main points to note in the three events pertaining to actresses—the use of women to play female roles and the fact that all three theatres were public theatres. There was thus possibly a tradition for the use of women, albeit of easy virtue, in theatre in India. Second, there was also an idea that the added attraction of women would bring in many more people to buy tickets to watch plays. In the second and third attempts that these two points were factered in the example of Lebedeff's theatre led the way. So if one has to examine the entry of the actress on stage in Calcutta one has to start with Lebedeff and Bengally Theatre. Brojendranath Bandopadhyay, who discussed this episode in 1933, refuses in the first line of his book to draw any connection with the regular performance of Bengali plays on stage in Calcutta from 1873 and the Bengally Theatre of 1795, since the proprietor of the latter and the director/playwright was not a Bengali.[2] But from his discussion and the quotes of Lebedeff one can see how Lebedeff became interested in translating two English plays, *The Disguise* and *Love is the Best Doctor* into Bengali and then was further encouraged by the offer of Goloknath Das, his linguist, to bring in performers of both sexes to the theatre. It can only be a matter of conjecture as to what gave the idea of bringing in women to perform since that is not discussed. A few years earlier, Amarendranath Roy translated the news of Lebedeff's theatre from Buckland's *Dictonary of Indian Biography* in the Bengali literary magazine *Basanti*.[3] Thereafter, it was also discussed in the *Calcutta Review* by G.A Grierson in English, followed a discussion by Sailendra Nath Mitra and Shyamaprasad Mukhopadhyay.[4] This explains why all writers in English and Bengali post-1921 had to discuss Lebedeff's theatre before they discussed contemporary Bengali theatre. Hemendranath Dasgupta in his discussion on the origin of Indian theatre first published in 1933, spoke of the use of performers of both sexes in the Sanskrit plays of ancient times and adds that the reputation of both, who were most often husband–wife, 'was rather low in society; actresses often led immoral lives . . . therefore Manu, the great Legislator, imposes only a small penalty in cases of adultery with actor's wives . . .'.[5] Since the arrival of Lebedeff coincided with the translation projects of the Asiatic Society and Lebedeff was himself a Sanskrit scholar, it is possible that he came to know about these ancient performances. Also, if in musical performances the women from north India were already seen in Calcutta as Hemendranath points out quoting *Bangadarshan* (1289 BS, 1882)[6] then Goloknath Das probably knew of such performers whom he could bring to Lebedeff for training in modern drama. Besides as Hemendranath Dasgupta points out there was 'nothing surprising about it' since 'Mrs Bristow's name was in the lips of every European of the settlement and the Calcutta Theatre was then in its full reputation with artists of both sexes'.[7]

Lebedeff's theatre saw two performances in 1795 and 1796 and from his writing and the high prices of the tickets[8] it is evident that the plays were very successful. But after the theatre by Lebedeff was destroyed by fire[9] there was a long gap before another Bengali play was performed. These years were crucial because Western education had been introduced and the Hindu College had been established. A sea change occurred in Bengali taste and culture. There was a conscious move away from what was characterized as popular culture[10] and towards a formulation of a culture suitable to the new Western-educated elite. This was true both of written as well as performing art. New taste created new vernacular literature, the music and lyrics of Bengali songs were re-moulded and there were attempts to sanitize the performing arts. The very popular Jatra (a drama with songs but without scenes or curtains or stage and audience sitting on three sides) was decried as unsophisticated in comparison to theatre, so much so that Jatra had to remodel itself to suit the standards of the new urban taste from 1821.[11] Besides change in content, there was concentration on the improvement of music through the influence of Hindustani Classical music. From 1849, a new Jatra started, *Nanda Biday*, where women trained in singing performed along with 'respectable' men.[12] This new-style Jatra became popular at a time when there were no Bengali plays being performed on stage. By way of tracing the different performances which preceded modern Bengali theatre, Hemendranath Dasgupta points out that performance by women were not the norm in the Jatras or the folk theatres in the days before the Maratha raids and the coming of the baijis into Bengal. Only then did women start singing Bengali kirtans and the Jatras were modernized to use women. He quoted in *The Hindu Intelligence* dated 26 March 1849 to show that two girls, especially Chhidam, charmed the audience by their songs in *Nanda Biday Jatra* by the Glee Club.[13]

The period from 1796 to 1831 also saw the co-existence of English theatres in Calcutta where women performed regularly, like the Sans Souci, Theatre Royal of Mrs Lewis, and Opera House and Garrison Theatre. These theatres were visited by Bengalis too and the acting styles of the actresses were closely studied and analysed.[14] From the middle of the century, theatres were established in many schools and private theatres in the houses of the elite where plays in English were staged, like the Hindu Theatre of Prasanna Kumar Thakur (1831), Hindu College (1837), David Hare Academy (1853), Metropolitan Academy (1852), and the Oriental Theatre (1853). In the last mentioned theatre, training in acting was given by an English lady, Madame Elise, and in 1854 another lady, Mrs Grieg acted with the 'Hindu gentlemen' as newspaper reports show. Contemporary writings express dissatisfaction at plays not being performed in Bengali despite the fact that so much organizational skill was evident in the English plays. There was no outcry at an English actress performing with impressionable young men. Indian women were not only banned from the stage, they were also banned from the audience though there was always mention of the presence of English ladies in the audience in the contemporary editorials and reviews.

Then came another major event in the history of Bengali theatre. In 1833, a theatre established by Nabin Chandra Basu of Shyambazar saw the performance of *Bidyasundar* with both actors and actresses. The interesting feature of this theatre was that sets depicting different scenes of the play were constructed in different parts of the room with chairs set for audiences in front. So as the play progressed, the audience moved from scene to scene along with the action of the play.[15] The newspaper reports after the 1835 performance were ecstatic. The *Hindu Pioneer* (October 1835) said that a thousand people enjoyed the night-long performance and a veiled threat was made that anyone wanting the improvement of the Indian culture was bound to be happy at the inclusion of Hindu women in theatre. The mental strength of the uneducated actresses was lauded and the need for women's education highlighted. As the writer said, 'Ought not the very sight of these girls induce our native visitors present on this occasion to spare no time in educating their wives and daughter? Had this girl, who has made such a capital figure on the stage, been educated in the study of her vernacular language, I, as a Hindu, beg my countrymen to consider how her talents would have shown! Was not her ingenuity, though she spoke only by rote, sufficient to convince those who charge Nature for being partial to men that Hindu females are as well fitted to receive education as their superior lords? . . .'[16] Unfortunately this was only one side of the coin. A debate started decrying the use of prostitutes in the performance in a number of newspapers. In reply to a letter in the *Harkaru* (28 October 1835), where a critic under the pseudonym of 'a Lover of Truth', made some severe remarks against the above article in the *Hindu Pioneer*, a letter to the Editor of the *Hindu Pioneer* was published on 7 November 1835. Here, the writer who called himself 'Z', says that it is unfair that the Native theatre has been called immoral because women of public character are seen on the stage. He asks people to look at the theatres of Italy, France, Germany, etc., where though the same phenomenon is visible, society is tolerant. Though the Editor of the *Hindu Pioneer* called the entire debate an excess of 'alarm and frenzy, ludicrously disproportionate to the cause',[17] and though the *Englishman and Military Chronicle* derided the conservative attitude of the *Hindu Pioneer*,[18] the admonitions served their purpose. The use of actresses stopped for the next 37 years.

Unlike in the previous gap (1796–1833) when no evidence of the performance of a Bengali play is seen, the interregnum between 1835 and 1872 was a gap of a different kind. Though women were no longer seen to perform on stage as a result of a new sense of moral righteousness, society became very vocal not only about the parading of 'bad' or 'fallen' women on stage but about theatre as a whole—the quality and content of the plays that were staged, the impact of theatre on impressionable youth, etc. It was as if an awareness of women as actresses had emerged and anyone writing on theatre had to comment on it, whether in approval or condemnation. This period saw a boom of private theatres in the houses of the rich, cultured and the elite in Calcutta and larger towns of Bengal where plays in Bengali were performed. The time was not yet ripe for staging plays for the benefit of the common people. The audience of the plays in the private theatres was exclusively upper-class educated Hindu Bengali men. There was no mass involvement which may be one reason why this type of theatre did not last long.

These private amateur theatres were established from around 1857, where Bengali plays were performed. In all these theatres young men or boys (referred to as 'juvak' in the different writings) performed in women's roles in the presence of the elite of Bengali society. Rimli

Bhattacharya in her Introduction to her translation of Binodini Dasi's autobiography *Amar Kotha* (*My Story*), says that female roles were invariably played by men and less frequently by boys.[19] Girish Ghosh however repeatedly uses the word 'balak' as actors in women's roles. Theatres were established in the houses of Kaliprasanna Sinha in 1856, Ashutosh Deb and Ramjoy Basak in 1857, Gadadhar Seth and Narottam Pal in 1858, Belgachhia Natyashala by the Rajas of Paikpara in 1858, the Jorasanko Tagore family in 1859, the Pathuriaghata Tagore family in 1865, Sobhabazar Private Theatrical Society in 1865 and Bowbazar Banganatyalaya in 1868. What is noticeable in the writing of this period is that there is always a *presence* of the actresses even when they were absent in reality. They appear constantly in the minds of the audience and critics. The reviews of these plays which appeared immediately after the performances offered detailed discussions of how well or badly the young men acted as women. Often there are comments that it was imperative that the theatre owners should invest in more good-looking men because they do not look feminine enough. In almost all the plays the singing is criticized. In 1859, after the staging of the play *Bibaha Bibhrat* at the Metropolitan Theatre, *The Bengal Harkaru* and the *Indian Gazette* said that many members of the audience suggested that women should perform in the female character roles.[20] In 1866, in *The Bengalee*, Girish Ghosh wrote a review of the play, *Bidya Sundar* performed at the house of Jotindra Mohon Tagore at Pathuriaghata. He concluded by saying that, 'When we left we only wished that the female characters could be represented by women; for all the time we were painfully alive to the demoralizing tendency of boys and younger men throwing themselves into the attitude, the gestures, motions and even the voluptuousness of women. But as under existing circumstances of native society it is not possible to have any but courtesans to join the Corps Dramatique, we must choose the lesser of the two evils.'[21]

Michael Madhusudan Dutta, poet and dramatist, had very distinct views on the theatre. He was closely associated with the Belgachhia Theatre under the Rajas of Paikpara and Pathuriaghata Banganatyalaya under Jotindra Mohon Tagore and his letters convey his interest in them. He wrote one play after the other for performance in the theatres. In a letter to Keshab Ganguly, whom he revered as 'my Garrick', he speaks of a new romantic tragedy, *Krishna Kumari*, written by him in which he talks of introducing very few female characters so as to 'leave no loophole for our Manager to escape through. . . . If the Chota Raja should grumble about the females, please tell him I would undertake to find 3 out of the 4!'.[22] That Michael preferred women to perform female roles is also testified to by Girish Chandra Ghosh who says that in 'Krishna Kumari' Michael expressed dissatisfaction that women could not perform in female roles. The young boys who acted in these parts could not sing in a woman's voice and so playback singing became necessary which hampered the literary value of the play.[23] This point that Girish Ghosh made on behalf of Michael Madhusudan is interesting because it shows that playback singing was performed by women. Society had accepted the presence of women singers possibly because they were not in intimate physical contact with the male actors in public just as society accepts, however unwillingly, the presence of the prostitute and entertainer but never feels threatened by them. The moral embargo on actresses on stage was not applied to female talent in other forms of performing art. During major festivals and important occasions in the houses of the respectable and rich of Calcutta, famous singers/dancers like Mejibai, Gyanada, Basanta, Sarala Sundari and others, performed at 'Mehfils' or 'Kirtans'.[24] As Girish Ghosh pointed out most of the kirtan singers and dancers were prostitutes but there was no real hatred for them. It was only towards theatre that their fingers were raised.[25]

It is interesting that none of the enlightened men of Bengal who were deeply involved in reforms for the uplift of women considered the theatre as a professional alternative to the women who were stigmatized as 'fallen' by society. Even the Tagore family at Jorasanko which served as a beacon for women's liberty did not bring in women of any type, respectable or otherwise, to perform in plays despite the fact that they were performed before private invited audience. The Jorasanko Natyashala advertised for a competition in 1865 for dramas on various subjects. One was 'The Hindoo females: their condition and helplessness' and the prize money for this topic was the highest. Yet, during the performance all the roles were acted by men. It was only later that the women of the Tagore family and family friends created a stir in the conservative society by performing in plays at Jorasanko and later Santiniketan.

The history of Bengali theatre up to 1872 was not uninterrupted because it was dependent on private initiative and uncertain funding. From 1870 repeated onwards, demands appeared in the newspapers and magazines for public theatres for the benefit of the masses. One of the earliest voices was that of Michael Madhusudan who in a letter to Rajnarayan Bose in 1859, noted with regret that a National Theatre had not yet been established to regulate national taste.[26] Along with the demand for regular and organized performances in newspapers there occasionally appeared demands to induct actresses in the female roles. The newspaper reviews were no longer reticent about their criticism of the performance of female roles. In *Nabanatak* by Ramnarayan Tarkaratna, the review in *Somprakash* said that the actor in Sabitri's role looked more like a eunuch than a woman.[27]

In 1872, the Bengal Theatre was established by Sarat Chandra Ghosh and Pyarimohon Roy in its own premises. On the advice of Michael, four actresses were employed. According to Amritalal Bose's *Memoirs*, Michael promised to write a new play for the theatre if actresses were used.[28] The four women were local prostitutes—Jagattarini, Golaap, Elokeshi, and Shyama who acted in Michael's play *Sarmistha*. Iswar Chandra Vidyasagar who was in the committee of the Bengal Theatre was opposed to the idea and resigned but Umesh Ch. Dutta, Biharilal Chatterjee, Haridas Das, Girish Ghosh, Debendranath Mitra, Batu Babu, Priya Nath Bose, Akshoy Kumar Majumdar and Satyabrata stayed on. Vidyasagar seems reticent on this matter though he was aware that many of the prostitutes were unfortunate Hindu widows whom he was trying to rehabilitate through remarriage.[29]

Though the National Theatre first opened the door to the public through the sale of tickets, they did not over the performance of the first five to six plays, use women in female roles. It was Bengal Theatre in 1873, which employed Jagattarini, Golaap, Elokeshi and Shyama, Unfortunately the person who had most vociferously argued in favour of the use of actresses for the plays and in fact had offered to find at least three women to perform in the plays as well as write a play for them, died before the actresses could be used. So when the Bengal Theatre opened with his play *Sarmistha* it was for the benefit of his young sons who had been left in financial distress. As a matter of fact, with the introduction of the actresses Iswar Chandra Vidyasagar, the noted philanthropist, educator and advocate of widow remarriage ended his association with the theatre, of which he had been an enthusiastic patron.

On the night of the 16 August, two of the employed actresses came on stage as Debjani and Sarmistha's companion. There was trepidation in the newspapers regarding the new step and some said that since actresses had not been used for so long, Bengal theatre should step cautiously since society was not yet ready. And the managers should not 'stoop down to the level of the jatrawalas' (*Hindu Patriot*); one said that it was a tragedy that gentlemen were being seen with prostitutes (*Bharat Samskar*). There was even a protest against the presence of some Brahmo ladies in the audience because it was unseemly that they should see the acting of prostitutes (*Sadharani*). Though there was an improvement in the standard of performance, it could not compensate for the loss of moral uprightness of society. Monomohon Basu said in *Madhyastha*, that it was a sad time when instead of concentrating on social reforms for women, society was enjoying the performance of prostitutes on stage. It was specially tragic that the capital city should set such a bad example.[30]

Around the same time, in 1872, the National Theatre had been established but initially they did not use actresses. The response to the theatre was however very warm, especially because it was said that this theatre aimed at the improvement of society through performances for the masses. After the performance of *Nildarpan*, one critic, in *Halisahar Patrika*, said that the performance would be even better if actresses could be brought into the theatres which should not depend on prostitutes just because they were available. It was necessary that educated women be brought to the theatre.[31] In the next performance of *Jamai Barik* too women were not used and *National Paper* on 18 December 1872, advised the theatre against employing actresses. Society was going through an evolution and public opinion was not yet mature enough for it.[32] In 1873, Girish Chandra Ghosh joined the National Theatre and here, when Michael's *Krishna Kumari* was performed, no actresses were used. Soon afterwards, this theatre was split into the National Theatre and the Great National Theatre. In 1872, the Oriental Theatre too did not employ actresses.

It was on 17 September 1874 that for the first time five actresses—Kadambini, Kshetramoni, Jadumoni, Haridashi, and Rajkumari— were employed by the Great National Theatre. Girish Ghosh wrote that they were forced to do so because they were facing stiff competition from the Bengal Theatre. The numbers of the audience had dropped. Though Raj Krishna Roy wasted a lot of money on trying to find better boys, they were simply not good enough for the roles.[33]

From 1874, performance by actresses became more or less permanent though for a long time the debate about moral impact continued. As late as 1900, a defensive note is discernable in the writing of Girish Ghosh. He implores the enlightened men of Bengal to offer constructive suggestions rather than simply criticize or express disgust. He pointed out that the theatre owners did not use prostitutes out of any specific motive but because no 'respectable' woman would come forward to join the theatre. He argued that this was a universal problem and even in Europe at one time, only prostitutes were available for the theatre. In reply to a letter written by the headmaster of a school to the editor of *Rangalay*, Girish Ghosh wrote that the allegation against actresses, that they were enticing young boys away from their studies by leering at them or making overtures from the stage, was false. For a good performance it was imperative that the actresses face the audience and if there was any eye contact it was totally accidental and if any impressionable youth was impressed by the beauty and allure of an actress, then the audience was to blame and not the actresses. If they had been really impure, how could they have performed the purest characters so realistically and how could their art been blessed by Sri Ramkrishna.[34] He even recalls the story of an old man who on his deathbed asked his son to call a stage actress to the house so that he could die after listening to the prayer songs of the popular plays.[35]

From the 1870s, the reaction to actresses performing on public stage took another form. A number of women are seen to write plays meant for performance in the theatre. In 1871, Kamini Debi wrote *Usha Natak*, in 1872 Laksmimoni Debi wrote *Chira Sanyasi*, a social drama, in 1875 Sukumari Dutta (Golaap) a leading actress of the time wrote *Apurba Sati*, in 1879 Swarna Kumari Debi wrote *Basanta Utsav* for performance on stage. Two anonymous works were written in 1880 for the stage, *Agomoni* and *Bijoya* in 1880, in the same year, Sarala Sundari wrote *Surendra Sarala*, and Monomohini Debi wrote *Binod Kanan*. Many more plays were written at the turn of the century.[36]

These dramatic works, memoirs written by the actresses themselves or by ghostwriters [Binodini Dasi, *Amar Katha*, 1912,[37] Tinkadi Dasi, *Abhinetrir Kotha* (with the help of Upendranath Bidyabhushan)],[38] as well as articles in the leading journals by contemporary women focus on their reactions to the performances, the hopes and aspirations of nineteenth and twentieth century women and their limitations. How the actresses dealt with their inherent drawbacks to fight for their position in a highly competitive world, what the reactions of the contemporary world and women in particular to performance by actresses were, how the actresses in an eternal search for financial security compromised their art and how they strove to achieve an identity which transcended their birth is the story that kept Bengali society agog for the next century.

Notes

1. Gerasim (Herasim) Lebedeff, Introduction to *A Grammar of Pure and Mixed Dialects (1801),* quoted in Brojendranath Bandopadhyay, *Bangiya Natyashalar Itihas 1795–1876*, Calcutta: Bangiya Sahitya Parishad, 6th edn., 1991, pp. 14–15, in Bengali. Hemendranath Dasgupta discusses Lebedeff's theatre and all discussions on it in detail in *The Indian Theatre*, New Edition and Reprint, New Delhi: Gyan Publishing House, 2009, pp. 220–38. Reprint of the first page of Lebedeff's book and the programme cover for the second night of the play *The Disguise* can be seen in Sudipto Chatterjee, *The Colonial Staged: Theatre in Colonial Calcutta*, Oxford: Seagull Books, 2007, pp. 29–30.
2. Brojendranath Bandopadhyay, op. cit., p. 14.
3. Basanti, 22nd Jaishtha, 1921 quoted in Abinash Chandra Gangopadhyay, *Girish Chandra: Banga Natyashalar Itihas Sambalito* (1st pub. 1927), Calcutta: Dey's Publishing, 1977, p. 45.
4. Ibid.
5. Hemendranath Dasgupta, op. cit., p. 85.
6. Ibid., p. 122.
7. Ibid., p. 235.
8. Brojendranath Bandopadhyay, op. cit., pp. 16–17.
9. Discussion on the alleged sabotage which led to the fire in Sudipto Chatterjee, op. cit., pp. 33–5.
10. Sumanta Banerjee, *The Parlour and the Streets*, Calcutta: Seagull Books, 1989, pp. 153–66.
11. Brojendranath Bandopadhyay, op. cit., pp. 8–10.
12. Ibid.
13. Hemendranath Dasgupta, op. cit., p. 127. This is endorsed by Brojendranath Bandopadhyay, op. cit., p. 21.
14. Girish Ghosh, *Girish Racanabali*, ed. Rathindra Nath Roy and Devipada Bhattacharya, Calcutta: Sahitya Samsad, 3rd edn., 1991.
15. Abinash Ch. Gangopadhyay, Girish Chandra, op. cit., p. 46.
16. Quoted in Brojendranath Bandopadhyay, op. cit., p. 23.
17. Ibid., p. 26.
18. Ibid., p. 7.
19. 'Introduction', Binodini Dasi's *My Story and My Life as an Actress*, ed. and tr. Rimli Bhattacharya, Delhi: Kali for Women, 1998, p. 11.

20. Brojendranath Bandopadhyay, op. cit., p. 51. It was performed at the premises of the Hindu Metropolitan College but was organized by Ramgopal Mullick of Chitpore.
21. *Rangabhumir Itihas*, op. cit., p. 7.
22. Letters, Michael Madhusudan Datta, *Madhusudan Racanabali*, ed. Kshetra Gupta, Delhi: Sahitya Samsad, 1984, p. 569.
23. Pauranik Natak, *Girish Racanabali*, op. cit., p. 734.
24. Sumanta Banerjee, *Asruta Kanthaswar*, Calcutta: Subarnarekha, 2002, p. 29.
25. *Girish Racanabali*, op. cit., vol. I, pp. 735–6, first published in Rangalay, 17th Falgun, 1307 BS.
26. *Madhusudan Racanabali*, op. cit., p. 545.
27. Brojendranath Bandopadhyay, op. cit., pp. 69, 105.
28. Quoted in Brojendranath Bandopadhyay, op. cit., p. 102.
29. Iswar Chandra Vidyasagar, *Vidyasagar Granthavali*, ed. Suniti Kumar Chattopadhyay, Brojendranath Bandopadhyay and Sajanikanta Das, Vidyasagar Smriti Samrakshan Samiti, Delhi: Ranjan Publishing House, 1938, pp. 181–7. There is no mention of his rejection of actresses in his letters. *The Selected Letters of Vidyasagar*, ed. Santosh Kumar Adhikari, Calcutta:Vidyasagar Research Centre, 1985.
30. Brojendranath Bandopadhyay, op. cit., pp. 156–63.
31. Ibid., pp. 115–16.
32. Ibid., p. 117.
33. Girish Racanabali, op. cit., vol. I, p. 736.
34. Abhinetrir Samalochana, *Girish Racanabali*, op. cit., vol. III, pp. 823–7.
35. *Girish Racanabali*, op. cit., vol. I, p. 736.
36. Usha Chakraborty, *Condition of Bengali Women around the Second Half of the 19th Century*, Calcutta: Bardhan Press, 1963.
37. This was first published in 1912 then a new edition as *Amar Kotha ba Binodinir Kotha*, in 1913, then published as *Amar Kotha*, eds., Saumitra Chattopadhyay and Nirmalya Acharya in 1964 and then revised by the same editors as *Amar Kotha O Onyanya Racana* in 1971 and then revised and enlarged edition, Calcutta: Subarnarekha, 1984.
38. Reprinted in *Shatabdir Natyachinta* (*A Collection of Essays on Bengali Theatre*), ed. Debashish Majumdar and Sekhar Samaddar, Calcutta: A. Mukherjee and Company Private Ltd., 2000, pp. 86–94.

2

TRAINING OF THE ACTRESSES AND BLOSSOMING OF THEIR TALENT

SIMULTANEOUS WITH THE rise of the curtain on professional theatre in 1872 came the entry of the actresses. Their entry was a stormy one accompanied by both accolades and stern criticism. The fact that the only women available for the stage were from the prostitute quarters stirred the sensibilities of the 'respectable' society. Other than rudimentary artistic training, not much was expected from these women, and yet the returns were brilliant. This chapter sketches this picture of the actresses who were brought to the stage reluctantly, was considered a necessary evil, yet who managed to ably fulfil the role assigned to them. It also traces the tensions and contradictions in their career and life since they never really got their due. The actress remained a good student, a brilliant performer yet was never able to exceed the 'lead' actor in the choice of roles, monetary matters or in fame. She was also subordinated by her 'loyalty' to her mentor or patron and this loyalty in her career and personal life often hindered her ambition. The position of the actress always remained subordinate in this early period of the professional stage (1872–1920) known as the Actors' Theatre in contrast to the Producers' Theatre in the post-1920s.

Initially there was very little expectation of good performance from the actresses since it was known that they were from backward and uneducated sections. But when night after night the actresses performed brilliantly in different plays, the praise of the critics became unstinted. How could these prostitutes become transformed into the characters of 'noble women' or 'Heavenly Goddesses'. Though they were uneducated, they were able to interpret the complexities of human nature and even portray Anglicized Bengali characters with English-based dialogues. They acted with aplomb in historical tragedies portraying strong and complicated characters.

To be recognized as a top-level actress, she had to be good in enunciation in her dialogue delivery. Speech defect was the real bugbear. The 'sh' was pronounced as 's' and the improper positioning of syllables or uttering the word with broken syllables were the chief defects. Another problem arose from some specific dialect-based speech defects. Binodini, Tinkadi Dasi or Tarasundari became successful and famous because of their correct pronounciation and dialogue delivery.

To be a great and popular actress, she had to be not only good in acting but also had to be a good performer excelling in singing and dancing. Binodini was a legend during and after her time but even she was criticized for not being 'really good in singing'. She is said to have had to compensate with her acting in the musicals. But despite her fame, she was not exempted from portraying characters in which singing was essential since all plays included songs sung by the female characters to attract the audience. The playwrights included songs not really required in the script to gain popularity at the box office. Dancing according to Girish Ghosh was not a part of the theatre in the initial years. In an essay called 'Rongaloye Nepen-Banganatyashalay nrittyashiksha o tahar kromobikash', Girish writes that the occasional khemta of the farces were transformed into attractive dance sequences with the introduction of formal dance training.[1]

For the actress there was always the need to transcend her background—not only through the performances but even offstage. Debnarayan Gupta recalls a story of the Star Theatre where the custom was that actresses would be brought from their homes to the theatre in a closed carriage and would enter the theatre veiled. One summer the actresses decided to relieve the heat by keeping the doors open while the carriage was travelling through the streets of Calcutta. When the manager Amar Dutta heard of this he immediately dismissed the coachman and roundly scolded the scared actresses that the only reason people came to the theatre was because a world far removed from their own was created in the theatre. When they realized that without costume and makeup the actresses were such ordinary creatures everyone would be disillusioned. . . .[2]

Most of the actresses came to the theatre at a very tender age. Binodini came to the stage at the age of eleven, Tarasundari at nine, Tinkadi at eight, etc. Besides being young, they came from backgrounds steeped in penury and illiteracy. Yet they were expected to perform in important roles as sons or daughters of socially-leading characters or even lead roles in mythological or musical plays like that of Lav Kush or Prahlad or Nemai. Naturally they required training. They were taught by the legendary actors of the time such as Girish Ghosh, Ardhendu Sekhar Mustafi or Amritalal Bose or Amritalal Mitra. The idea began to circulate among the actors/producers, playwrights, critics and leading men of the time that if these young inexperienced girls could put up such fine performances, what could they not achieve with education. A large number of journals of the time contain articles expressing this sentiment. In *Nachghar,*[3] the editor Nalinimohon Roychowdhury said that it is true that while actresses do not really need to have school education, an overall education definitely improves the quality of the mind and hence performance. The editor believes that Tinkadi despite being a star was too dependent on training. This was reflected in her performance—when she trained under a great teacher her performance was outstanding, while with mediocre training her performance too suffered. An offshoot of this view was the idea that the theatre had got a bad name for itself because in it the sons of the 'respectable' middle-class families were associated intimately with these women of 'low morality'. Education would improve their minds and bring respectability to the profession of acting.

For others it was more specifically training in the performing arts that was the concern. It was felt that in comparison with the English theatre, whether in England or Calcutta, the Bengali stage was too unprofessional. On one hand, improvement was necessary in the writing of the plays for which a large number of literary works were initiated in that period, and on the other hand there was a call for proper training of performers following the styles of acting popular in English theatre. The leading journals on drama like *Nachghar* or *Sisir* contain editorials and sections on the analysis of the acting styles of contemporary British actors. Nirmalendu Lahiri wrote in *Sisir* that the careers and lives of foreign actors should be read to realize how much effort they put in to reach perfection.[4] Books on performances were read and the discussions on the most popular actors like Garrick for the performance of King Lear, Keene for Iago, Kemble, Henry Irving for Shylock, Toole, Mrs Siddons for Lady Macbeth, Sara Bernhard for Cordelia, etc., are noticeable. In a letter written to Amritalal Basu, Henry William Moreno pointed out that modern actors did not seem to follow the real rules of acting. When Moreno was a young actor they had to spend days and nights studying a single play before making an attempt at performing it.[5] Gyanendranath Chakraborty serially discusses the performances of English stage actresses in *Natyamandir.*[6]

A number of essays by the leading playwrights and dramatists of the time contained advice and instructions to actors, directors and stage managers on the total performance including acting, singing, dancing, stage sets, costume, lights, etc. The dramatist Dwijendralal Roy was not content simply to write plays to fill the lacuna. He was keen that they should also be performed well and scientifically like the theatres he watched in England. He wrote *Abhinetar Kartavya* (*Duties of an Actor*) which came out in 1910 in *Natyamandir*[7] in which he wrote extensively about the ideals of acting. The motive of acting is to portray the incidents of the play before the audience since there are very few readers who have the ability to visualize a drama just by reading it. There are three means of portraying a play—scenery/backdrop, costume and acting. Acting had three parts—oration/dialogue delivery, facial expression and body language. The delivery of dialogue by the actor should be such that the entire audience should be able at all times to hear the dialogue clearly. The actor must be careful that even when the dialogue demands a low voiced delivery it should never be so soft that the audience misses some words, even if that meant that for the front rows the delivery was unnaturally loud. Dwijendralal considered Girish Ghosh's deep voice as ideal for an actor. Second, modulation was an art which Dwijendralal felt had not been successfully developed in the country, where excessive shouting was interpreted as good acting. In reality, only anger is indicated by a loud voice. Third the pace of dialogue delivery should be determined according to the meaning of the dialogue, when one is thoughtful or when one is awed or when one wants to convey something significant, one speaks slowly and when one has to indicate urgency and lack of time or excitement, one speaks fast. The actor should be aware of these rules. Fourth, it is sometimes necessary to raise or lower the voice gradually, especially when there are repetitions or when there is a danger of the acting becoming boring. Finally, emphasis is an important part of dialogue and an actor needs to be trained properly in this. The expert in the art of emphasis according to Dwijendralal was Ardhendu Shekhar Mustaphi.

Controlling facial expressions is a difficult exercise and an actor has to accomplish the art if he has to express the myriad of human emotions. Make-up should be skilful so that a face appears flushed or pale according to the needs of the script. Body language generally conveys thoughts, sometimes complementing speech and sometimes going beyond it. The actions of an actor should be suitable to the dialogue, the character and the situation of the play and it should not be artificial or overdone. Of course, sometimes acting acts as a commentary on the play when it conveys to the audience an interpretation of the play which would otherwise elude the audience. But in general, the acting should aim to be as lifelike as possible.

Articles in the leading journals stressed the need for the overall training of the actress. An article in *Nachghar*[8] stressed the importance of voice modulation. Even in a small role, Nirodasundari stands out because of the way she expresses emotion—without shouting, yet every word was audible even in the last row of the gallery. *Sisir* regrets that because of the different kinds of dances an actress performs in the different roles, she is unable to master the genuine art form. The chorus numbers were especially disreputable. There are some articles which also speak of the need for specialized training like sword-fighting and gymnastics. *Nachghar*[9] makes a comparison between the performance of sword-play in the English and Bengali stages. *Bangla*[10] speaks of the need to preserve the beauty of the actresses, through disciplined living and physical exercise. The tendency of the Bengali actress to put on weight has been deplored saying that it makes her fit only for comic roles. Besides, they show signs of age very early. Make-up can hide old age in actors but not in actresses.

A discussion in *Natyamandir* highlights the need for improvement in the costumes of the actresses. All the characters in different plays, whether mythological, historical or social, wore the same costumes. The worst were the companions of the lead actresses, called sakhis. They all wore the same sakhi suit. None of the actresses knew how to brighten their skin colour and used make-up in such an untrained and uniform manner that all actresses in different roles looked the same.[11]

This period has been referred to by the drama critics as the Actors' Theatre where the different styles of leading actors determined the acting style of the theatres to which they belonged. They taught their characteristic style to the other actors under their supervision. This meant that their teaching styles too were different. Abinash Ch. Gangopadhyay, Girish Ghosh's scribe, has made a comparative study of his teaching and that of Ardhendu Sekhar. Ardhendu Sekhar, who directed plays written by others, demonstrated to his students the way he perceived a character and then asked them to imitate him to their best ability. This did not leave much room for the originality of the artist but for the average performer the work was made simple. Girish Ghosh had a different philosophy. He first read the whole play to the troupe. The actors could now visualize all the roles in all their depth and significance. He then left the interpretation of the significant roles largely to the discretion of the leading actors. He only disciplined the natural talent of each actor.[12] Binodini, in her autobiography, also discussed the teaching style of Girish Ghosh. 'He had a wonderful teaching method: first he would explain the *bhave* (feel) of the role in question, then he asked me to memorize the lines. After this, he would, at his convenience come to our house . . . talk about numerous English actresses and works of famous English poets. . . .'[13] Girish Ghosh himself wrote in *Abhinoy O Abhineta* that acting was not simply training in how to render dialogue but a total education—to comprehend how the character is supposed to behave. He offers illustrations from the acting by famous English actors and actresses.[14] These references to English theatre could have been an attempt to create an atmosphere of respectability and legitimacy for the Bengali theatre. He wanted to show that though everywhere actresses are regarded as 'fallen women' yet their performances win all hearts. But the stigma was not so severe in England where a study shows that by the mid-nineteenth century, with the entry of the disciplined delicacy of Victorian sensibility, the profession of acting was becoming if not exactly respectable, at least a good deal more acceptable. Actresses like Lena Ashwell took over the management of the Kingsway Theatre in 1907 and in the next year the Actresses Franchise League was established to support the campaign for women's suffrage.[15]

According to some critics, it was the women who were more keen to learn the art of acting. They came from very backward backgrounds and they knew that they would need training to fit into the unfamiliar roles they had to play. The men however came from well-to-do and middle-class backgrounds and so felt too superior to learn anything new. According to Monomohon Goswami, it was this ignorance that proved to be the reason for the degeneration of theatre.[16]

Saurindramohon Mukhopadhyay wrote in 1921 after the performance of *Alamgir*, on 10 December, that Sisir Kr. Bhaduri was not only a great actor but also a wonderful teacher. 'The stage and performance has been dramatically transformed. Tarasundari, under Sisir's training was able to forget all the training she had received so long and perform in tune with Sisir as the Begum of Udipuri. Prova too as the princess Rupkumari of Rupnagar was stunning.'[17]

Sometimes these mentors were able to look into the future and save the situation through their foresight. There was an instant when Girish Ghosh apprehended that Binodini, even though at the height of her fame, could abandon the theatre and go into seclusion. He never let his apprehension become public but quietly started training Kironbala in the role of Rangini in *Bellick Bajar* as Binodini's understudy. When this training became public knowledge people began to criticize Girish since Binodini was everybody's darling and everyone thought that Kironbala would be a flop. But Girish was right on both counts. Binodini soon abandoned theatre and Kironbala was a success as Rangini and as Bishkha in *Rup o Sanatan* in 1887.[18]

There were many instances where actresses responded not simply to training but to an inner call. They were, on occasion, able to rise above their station in a way which no training, however superior, can teach. In descriptions of dedication of the actresses to theatre one notices ideas and actions extraneous to acting and sometimes far exceeding ordinary acting. Binodini's characteristic was her total involvement in the character she was portraying. She recalls one occasion when she was playing Prahlad, when she was so caught up in her part that she did not even notice that her clothes were on fire. Other actresses too were oblivious of the danger to their lives when they jumped into the fire while acting out 'jauhar' or 'sati'.[19] Binodini was also an expert in costume and make-up and frequently worked on her own. This skill was very helpful when she acted in two or three roles in the same play. Her concentration and dedication in the performance of the lead role in *Chaitanyaleela* brought the sage Sri Ramkrishna to the theatre and then to the Green Room to bless her. It not only brought a new dimension to Binodini's thoughts, but provided the balm of respectability to the much-maligned Bengali theatre.

Tinkadi recalls that she never refused to perform any role that was offered to her no matter how difficult the preparation might prove to be. So when Girish Ghosh asked her to perform Lady Macbeth's role replacing Pramada within five to six days of her joining Minerva, Tinkadi took up the challenge and in her words 'was able to justify

Girish's faith in me with the blessings of the *Natanath* Lord of Drama'. She also had the satisfaction of her mentor's praise at the end of her performance after a rigourous training by Girish. He said, 'After seeing your performance I feel that I have been justified writing this play. Let all Bengalis see that Bengali stage too has (great) actresses. That you would be able to perform so beautifully and flawlessly was beyond all my expectations.'[20]

Rabindranath Tagore always attended the performances of his plays in the public theatre. On one occasion he went to Natya Niketan to watch *Gora* and sat through four hours of the performance. He was very pleased with the performances of Rajlakshmi as Anandamoyee and Charubala as Lalita. He was stunned by the Sanskrit recitation of Charubala and when he heard that she was illiterate and took her salary by putting a thumb impression, he was truly amazed, as recalled his companion Charu Chandra Bhattacharya.[21]

It was very difficult when an actress had to perform two widely-differing roles. As Shambhu Chandra Mukherjee wrote in 1885 in *Reis and Raiyat*, about Binodini that it was a great trial for her to perform as Chaitanya and Bilashini since one was graceful and divine while the other was full of levity and flirtatious. He also presented a critical picture of the performances of Gangamoni, who was 'not a bad actress but wanted some paint on her person'. Obviously their dark complexion was hampering Mukherjee's full appreciation. Basantakumari too needed paint according to him and 'made such a miserable consort for the divine guru'. He was more complimentary about Bhunimoni and Kshetramoni. 'Bhunimoni no bad actress is a melodious nightingale who gives no small strength to a company dependent upon the support of a yatra loving community. Kshetramoni is a splendid actress equal to almost any comic business and possessing great declamatory powers for tragedy also.'[22]

Kusumkumari was uneducated but was able to perform creditably in English plays—as Lady Macbeth in *Macbeth* and as Lady Anne in *Richard III*. *Amrita Bazar Patrika* on 8 August 1917 wrote that 'the rendering of a Shakespearean scene in original English by a Bengali actress is a wonderful thing'. She was also outstanding in other ways. Not only was she a great performer—in acting and dancing, she performed with her partner Amarendranath Dutt in gramophone records and also was the first woman dance choreographer and trainer.[23]

Though love of acting made some actresses stick to their profession through thick and thin, others merely considered the stage a means of finding security under a rich patron and giving up acting would be automatic. Girish Ghosh, under whom all actresses, famous or not, would love to be trained, referred to this when he wrote about the difficulties faced by trainers in dramatic art due to the lack of professional training and the background of the actors and actresses, lack of infrastructure, lack of a tradition of theatrical talent and finally the absence of constructive and knowledgeable criticism. He considered it a great pity that 'just when an actress is educated in the art of dramatics after great effort, a "captain" (meaning a rich patron of theatre) carries her off'.[24]

NOTES

1. *Girish Racanabali*, vol.V, Calcutta: Sahitya Samsad, 1991, repr., pp. 335–40.
2. Devnarayan Gupta, *Natnatider Bichitra Kahini*, Calcutta: Grantha Prakash, 1964, pp. 11–12.
3. Third year, 4th samkhya, 3rd Asad, 1331 BS.
4. Nirmalendu Lahiri, 'Adhunik Abhinoy O Darshakdiger Kartabya', *Sisir*, 6th Baishakh, 1332 BS.
5. Arun Kumar Mitra, *Amritalal Basur Jibani O Sahitya*, Calcutta, Navana, 1970, p. 127.
6. Gyanendranath Chakraborty, 'Theaterer Katha', *Natyamandir*, 4th year, 2nd samkhya, 1320 BS.
7. Dwijendralal Roy, *Abhinetar Kartavya*, *Dwijendra Racanabali*, ed. Rathindra Nath Roy, Calcutta: Sahitya Samsad, 1985, 3rd edn., vol. I, pp. 710–12.
8. *Nachghar*, 21st samkhya, 13th Asad, 1331 BS.
9. *Nachghar*, 4th year, 7th samkhya, 23rd Asad, 1334 BS.
10. *Bangla*, 25th Baishakh, 1332 BS.
11. Monomohon Goswami, 'Kalavidyar Biparjoy', *Natyamandir*, 3rd year, 1st samkhya, Sravan, 1319 BS.
12. Abinash Ch. Gangopadhyay, *Girish Ghosh*, ed. Swapan Majumdar, Calcutta: Dey's Publishing, 1993, 2nd edn., pp. 422–3.
13. Binodini Dasi, *Amar Jiban*, tr. Rimli Bhattacharya, *My Story and My Life as an Actress,* Delhi: Kali for Women, 1998, p. 78.
14. *Girish Racanabali*, op. cit., vol. III, pp. 829–44.
15. Simon Trussler, *Cambridge Illustrated History of the British Theatre*, Cambridge: Cambridge University Press, 1994, p. 264.
16. Monomohon Goswami, 'Rangabhumi bhalobashilam keno', *Satabdir Natyachinta—Girish Ghosh theke Utpal Dutt*, ed. D. Majumdar and S. Samaddar, Calcutta: A. Mukherjee and Co. Pvt Limited, 2000, p. 114.
17. Quoted in Sankar Bhattacharya, *Natyacharya Sisirkumar*, Calcutta: D.M. Library, 1970, p. 51.
18. Debnarayan Gupta, *Banglar Natnati*, Calcutta: Sahityalok, 1985, pp. 125–6.

19. Binodini Dasi, 'Amar Abhinetri Jiban', *Rup O Ranga*, 1st year, 26th samkhya, 12th Baishak, 1332 BS.
20. Tinkadi Dasi, *Abhinetrir Katha*, written in association with Upendranath Bidyabhushan, repr. Shatabdir Natya, op. cit., p. 93.
21. Charuchandra Bhattacharya, Natoker Shilpi Rabindranath, *Satabdir Natyachinta*, op. cit., p. 162.
22. Quoted in H.N. Dasgupta, *The Indian Stage*, vol. III, Girish Centenary Edition, Calcutta: M.K. Dasgupta, 1944, p. 65.
23. Endnotes in Ramapati Dutta, *Rangalaye Amarendranath*, ed. Debjit Bandopadhyay, Calcutta: Dey's Publishing, 2004, p. 371.
24. Girish Ghosh, *Bartoman Rangabhumi*, Rangalaya, 1901 (1308 BS) 23rd Paus 1st year, 39th samkhya, repr. *Shatabdir Natyachinta*, op. cit., p. 3.

3

THE SKY WITHIN THEIR GRASP

Interpretation of Great Dramas

THE ACTRESSES HAD through their rigorous training under great mentors like Girish Chandra Ghosh and others like Ardhendu Sekhar and Amritalal Bose and repeated successful performances of plays adapted from great literature like that of Bankim Chandra Chattopadhyay or translations of world-famous works like the plays of Shakespeare, become adept at rendering great performances in all successful written dramas of the time. The mentors of the stage not only adapted popular literature but also wrote highly successful plays for the stage. This chapter, discusses performances by the actresses in the dramas of two great men of Bengali literature, Dwijendralal Roy and Rabindranath Tagore whose dramas became popular along with the other genres of literature, for which they are more famous. The response of public theatre to their dramas took paths different from those who were directly associated with it as directors, managers and playwrights. But though both Dwijendralal and Rabindranath entered public theatres as outsiders, the paths that their dramas took were not identical and the interpretation of their dramas by the actresses too did not occur in the same manner. Dwijendralal was from the beginning associated with the training process directly and so distortion of his work was less as compared to Rabindranath whose association with the theatre was never direct at least in the initial phase. In the latter's case, even indirect association through Dinendranath Tagore as music trainer occurred a decade from the time his plays were performed in the public theatre. So in the initial period at least his plays were totally at the mercy, so to speak, of the stalwarts of the theatre. What I would like to stress is that their dramas, even when they were not associated with the theatre directly, could not be ignored by those controlling public theatre because of the popularity they commanded. This was in spite of the fact that those closely associated with the theatre were writing very successful plays, totally adapted to fit the needs of the theatre.

Dwijendralal Roy came into direct association with the theatre a few years after the death of his wife in November 1903, though he was already present at the rehearsals of *Bahut Achha* the year before 18 January 1902. In fact, it was a matter of great distress among his friends that Dwijendralal, a man of moral integrity, was associating with the den of vices. But through his frequent visits to Classic during the performance of his farce *Tryahasparsha*, he realized, as testified to by his biographer that through training these unfortunate women would be able to rise above their backgrounds and be successful performers.[1] He believed that duality of morals was present in all human beings and if there was any desire in these women to repent their lack of morality and change their lifestyle through art, then it was the duty of all individuals to support them. On the other hand, those who believe that visiting a theatre which has been contaminated by these fallen women will destroy their character should lock themselves up in their homes since such feeble-minded and morally precarious men may err by just walking down the streets.[2] By then, he had already written six plays which were being performed regularly in the theatres. *Biraha* first performed in Star in November 1899 continued to be performed there between 1901 and 1909 for 34 performances, including a special performance on the evening before the coronation of King Edward VI.

Rana Pratap was the first drama that Dwijendralal wrote after his entry into the world of public theatre. In Star, Dwijendralal's *Rana Pratap* was launched on 22 July 1905 within three months of its publication in May 1905. The actresses performing in the play were Narisundari as Meherunnissa and Basantakumari as Daulaunnissa. It disloged the highly successful *Pratapaditya* of Kshirodeprasad Vidyabinode which had been running from 15 August 1903. As Aparesh Ch. Mukhopadhyay wrote in *Rangalaye Trish Bachhar*, the soft notes of *Rana Pratap* did not seem out of place in the hot seat that had been created by *Pratapaditya*. But the inclusion of the popular poem of Girish Ghosh, *Haldighater Yudhha* by the manager and director

Amritalal Bose, through the lips of some side characters in the play written by Dwijendralal in the stage adaptation was not liked by the dramatist. Dwijendralal broke off his connection with Star after the first night, on 22 July 1905.[3] Star's loss was Minerva's gain because while performances of *Rana Pratap* continued at Star for twenty-four nights till 1909, the rest of Dwijendralal's very popular plays were performed at Minerva. It is interesting that there was no performance in Star on 6 September 1905, in protest against Partition of Bengal by Lord Curzon and the play which recommenced its performance on 9 September was *Rana Pratap.* The advertisement in *Amrita Bazar Patrika* on 6 September said,

> Mourning at Star!!! / Partition of Bengal / No amusement at the / Star Theatre / on / Wednesday, 6 September / Amrita Lal Bose / Manager. On 9 September, another advertisement announced.

> Grand Dramatic Night! Rana Pratap! / Rana Pratap! Saturday / the 9 September at 9 p.m. / On the raising of the curtain the / recently written but already Universally popular / song by Babu Rabindranath Tagore 'Sonar Bangla, etc.' will be sung by all the / gentlemen vocalist of the company. . . .[4]

Though Dwijendralal disassociated himself from Star, his play could not be halted as it had already become very important in the context of the patriotic fervour gathering force among the theatre-going public. Also, ironically, the poem by Girish Ghosh was replaced by Rabindranath's song for the same reasons of popularity; but this time the topicality of the song, singing praises of the unity and beauty of Bangla was undeniable and the dramatist apparently had no objection.

Tarabai started performance in Unique Theatre on 31 October 1903 where Tarasundari performed in the role of Tarabai, making it a resounding success. However, the use of blank verse experimented on by Dwijendralal was 'rather jarring to the ears of the audience' after the 'musical notes of Girish Chandra's verse play' but 'due to the flow of events in the play and the powerful acting it was very successful'.[5] It was then performed seven times in Minerva from 25 December 1903. Kusumkumari performed the role of Tarabai. Minerva saw the performance of a large number of Dwijendralal Roy's plays regularly. Unlike Rabindranath's plays where names were changed or adaptations from his novels used (like *Raja Basanta Roy* or *Pratapaditya*) Dwijendralal's plays were performed in the original and the names were left unchanged, except in the case of *Bahut Achha* which was later changed and performed as *Prayaschitta* in Minerva. But since he was associated with both theatres he was probably consulted about the change of name. From *Rana Pratap* onwards, he was in fact writing plays keeping the theatre in mind, which is why he changed his dialogues from verse as in *Tarabai* to prose in *Rana Pratap* as it would be more 'natural'.[6]

When Dwijendralal left Star in protest against the addition of Girish Ghosh's poem at the beginning of *Rana Pratap* by the manager of Star, Amritalal Bose, and brought the play to Minerva, the direction to the actors and actresses was given by Ardhendu Sekhar and ironically Girish Ghosh, in the presence of the dramatist. A compromise was reached. This time the poem was not included in the voices of the actors—before the play started, Girish Ghosh himself recited the poem.[7] Obviously this was with the consent of the dramatist. *Rana Pratap* was first performed in Minerva on 29 July 1905 and the lead female roles went to Sushilabala as Meherunnissa, Bhushan Kumari as Ira, Tarasundari in both the roles of Daulatunnissa and Joshibai and Sudhirabala or Potol as Lakshmi. The reason for the performance of Tara in two roles on the first night is described very graphically by Aparesh Chandra. 'Daulatunnissa's role had been given to the late Kironbala. On the evening of the first performance we got the news that she had fallen ill. But we still did not realize that she would not come. The car which had gone to fetch her had not returned. We were getting ready and the concert had started playing when we got the news that she was so ill that she was unable to get up and so would not be able to come to the theatre. A pandemonium started in the green room. Soon after the second concert was played the curtain was raised. This was a competitive performance (with that of Star) and the sky had fallen on our heads. This was such a difficult role—who would stand up to perform so suddenly? On stage Prithviraj and Joshibai were performing their parts. Behind the wings Monomohonbabu, Mahendrababu and a few of us were conferring amongst us what would be done, what should be done. Then it was decided that only Tara could do it, if she agrees only then could the situation be saved. The programme was consulted and it was found that Joshibai and Daulatunnissa do not meet on stage. As soon as Tara came in to the green room after her performance as Joshibai, Monomohonbabu or Mahendrababu (don't remember exactly) told Tara that she would have to change into Daulatunnissa's dress very quickly. Tara was shocked into asking why but there was no time even to explain. She had heard of Kiron's illness so she could guess what had happened, because she knew that in theatre work such incidents happen. That night Tara performed both the roles in her inimitable way, both roles were perfect characterizations, totally different. No one realized the real reason and in fact most people in the audience thought that it was a ploy to win the competition.'[8]

There followed thirty-one performances of *Rana Pratap* over 1905–6 till the performance of *Durgadas* started. It was hailed as 'Mr. D.L. Roy's grand historical drama / Durgadas / or the Glory of Rajasthan / . . . sensational incidents—charming songs—graceful / dances!!!' Only one name was mentioned in the advertisement—that of 'Tincowrie Dassi as Mohamaya'.[9] When the performance started on 9 December 1906, the other lead roles were that of Sushilabala as Razia and Kusumkumari as Kamala. But the 3 November advertisement said that Kusumkumari was performing as Razia.[10] There were forty-nine performances till 1909 and one performance where the songs were performed. In fact, all Dwijendralal's plays contains numerous songs[11] all of which contributed to their great popularity. There is no doubt that this was kept in mind when the casting of the characters took place. In *Prayaschitta*, which was a changed *Bahut Achha*, launched in Minerva on 28 December 1907, Kusumkumari was Rebecca. Then on 18 March 1908 began *Nurjahan* (*The Light of the World*) and on the first show tickets worth Rs. 250 were sold. Prakashmani was Nurjahan.[12] Slight disturbances followed before the seventh performance since Star lured Amarendranath, who was performing as Jahangir in *Nurjahan* who returned Minerva's contract money and joined Star with Kusumkumari. However, not too much was affected since the advertisement for the tenth performance of *Nurjahan* on 16 May announced that its 'splendid success and magnificent / reception by the public have admittedly created / an epoch in the annals of the Indian Stage'.[13] It continued to run for thirty-five performances. Dwijendralal's experiment with dramatic opera, *Sohrab Rustom* opened in Minerva on 19 September 1908 with Sushilabala as Tamina and continued for fourteen performances. On 26 December 1908 *Mewar Patan* started, which Dwijendralal referred to as his first play on interaction.[14] The leading female roles were played by Sushilabala as Manasi, Prakashmoni as Satyabati, Hemantakumari as Kalyani and Sarojini (Nera) as Rani Rukmini. In the next year there were twenty-six performances of *Mewar Patan* in Minerva. *Shahjahan*, his next historical play in five acts started on 21 August 1909 in which the lead female roles were played by Sudhirabala (Potol) as Jahanara, Sushilabala as Piyara, Hemantakumari as Nadira, and Prakashmani as Mahamaya. The advertisement for the second performance to be held on 28 August in *Amrita Bazar Patrika* among its many superlatives and quotations from Shakespeare, announced

> . . . the tumultuous passions so vividly painted and so / faithfully represented the charming and soul—enrap- / turing songs of Peari Banu, the memorable dance / which cost Murad the throne of Hindusthan, the / dancing girls of Kashmere steering a boat and dis- / coursing sweet music from the boards and last / though not the least the national songs of 'Amar / Janma Bhumi', sung in chorus / by a score of charan boys with all / succeed in producing an impression which, it will / require a long time indeed to forget.[15]

There were eighteen performances in four months. As mentioned before, *Bahut Achha* was launched in Classic Theatre on 19 January 1902, with Kusumkumari as Rebecca, Pramadasundari as Sukeshini, Ranisundari as Subeshini, Kironbala as Suhasini, Binodini (Handi) as Subhasini and Aaya, Nagendrabala (Bunchi) as Indumoti, and Bhubaneshwari as Sarojini. It was unfortunate that just before the start of *Bahut Achha* Tarasundari left Classic because her demand for a pay increase was not granted. She joined Aurora theatre from 21 January 1902.[16] During the fourth performance of *Bahut Achha*, Jyotindra Mohon Tagore presented a gold medal to Amarendranath Datta 'in recognition of his services to the Bengali Stage'.[17] There were twenty-two performances of *Bahut Achha* in Classic, though midway Classic faced difficulties due to the abandonment of Classic by Girish Ghosh for non-payment of dues and refusal to launch Tagore's *Chokher Bali* as a play in October 1904 and then because Atul Chandra Roy was placed in Classic as Receiver by the Calcutta High Court. From 1905, Amarendranath, the proprietor of Classic and the main actor, was also made the Manager. After Tarasundari left, it was up to Kusumkumari to hold up the reins of Classic.

No plays of Dwijendralal were performed at City Theatre of Harrison Road or Aurora Theatre of Beadon Street. Unique Theatre which replaced Arora in Beadon Street was the first place where *Tarabai*, was performed with Tarasundari as Tarabai for fifteen nights. Tarasundari's fame as a heroine in Dwijendralal's plays was well-known. She was cast in the lead role as a strategy so that people would be encouraged to visit a new theatre instead of going to Minerva, since Tarasundari performing in a D.L. Roy *Durgadas* would have been a unique performance to behold. When Unique Theatre closed down in mid-1905, the actors and actresses of Arora and Unique formed the National Theatre taking over the lease of 9, Beadon Theatre. After a couple of performances of *Tarabai*, it was announced that *Durgadas* was to be performed, but the name of the author was not mentioned in the advertisements, possibly since on the same night Minerva too launched *Durgadas* with Dwijendralal's approval and support. Possibly this was some other play and not the same *Durgadas*, since in the list of characters, Tarasundari is Golina and Harimoti is Selina, characters who do not appear in Dwijendralal's *Durgadas*. But the audience would not know all the details and would undoubtedly be hoodwinked. It did have around twenty-five performances and so it was Tarasundari's acting prowess in a not famous play that triumphed. Only in the last two performances after Tarasundari left National to take *Riziya* of Monomohon Roy which she had already made famous wherever she went, to Kohinoor Theatre, was the lead character played by Tinkadi Dasi. Another competition is noticeable here. Following Amarendranath Datta who started the practice in Classic, here too the plays in book-form were offered during performances in 1908.

Not simply content to write plays to fill the lacuna of good plays for the theatre, Dwijendralal was keen that they should also be performed well and scientifically like the plays he watched in England. He wrote in *Abhinetar Kartabya* (*Duties of an Actor*) which came out in 1910 in *Natyamandir*,[18] what the ideals of acting were (see Chapter 2).

The Tagore family at Jorasanko acted as a path-breaker in many ways in Bengali society and not the least regarding culture and performing arts. Much before Rabindranath attained maturity and started writing drama, plays were performed in his house in which the whole family actively participated including women. This was undoubtedly an astonishing feature which set their family apart in Calcutta society since in the public theatre of the time (1872 onwards) the performance of female roles by actresses, who were unfortunately, yet necessarily, brought in from the red light areas, created sharp divisions of opinion in society about theatre and performance as a whole. Even if in the initial phase women did not join the Jorasanko theatrical performances, their active presence in the audience aroused wonder in the Bengali society.

In Rabindranath's family, not only did the men and women enjoy the amateur theatricals performed in a professional style in the Jorasanko Theatre but on special occasions they visited public theatres to watch the performance of Jyotirindranath Tagore's plays (*Asrumoti* in Bengal Theatre).[19] From 1877, women of the Tagore family participated in a performance of *Alikbabu* and this created a stir in society. Reflections of this was seen in the contemporary newspapers and journals which was further enhanced with the performance of *Raja O Rani* in 1889 when sanctity of family relations was broken in romantic pairing of characters and Bangabasi satirized it as 'Thakurbarir notun That'.[20] From 1881, Rabindranath started producing, directing and performing in his own plays in Jorasanko and then in Santiniketan and never was the performance of women for female roles an issue. Also, since most of his plays had a large component of music and dance, these performers had to be trained in both art forms which was rare in middle-class families but not in the Tagore family. Rabindranath, during his travels abroad, took the opportunity to study the production styles of the great performances and then applied them to his productions in Calcutta and Santiniketan. This new style of dress, backdrop, music which he adopted in the performance of plays under his production was different from the style of the public theatre. Even in the style of acting and delivery of dialogues, the difference was vast.

Most of the performances were performed either at Jorasanko or in the house of a family member or a close family friend to celebrate certain occasions. Sometimes, a public theatre was hired by the family for a special reason like raising funds for an organization like Stri Mandal or Adi Brahmo Samaj or the Poet's own Visva-Bharati or sometimes for charity during a natural calamity. These performances where the women of the household too participated were not entirely before an invited audience and tickets were sold to raise funds. The newspaper reports on these performances were surprisingly restrained generally referring to overall performances and not singling out any woman for either praise or criticism. But in 1923, when *Visarjan* was announced as being performed in Empire theatre with changes, the *Indian Daily News* remarked that 'the play which was written more than 30 years ago has been recast to a considerable extent, one or two minor characters being omitted and a new female character . . . introduced. This new character is an entirely novel conception. She will appear on the stage at intervals and sing in a way the clash of actions and emotion and furnishing them into a proper background. She is as it were, the spirit of the play personified. Her songs have been specially composed by the poet'.[21] The part was performed to perfection by Sahana Bose and two days later the same newspaper mentioned her valued contribution to the success of the play. 'She . . . supplied the connecting links with the aid of beautiful solos—the melody of their language and that of her voice casting a rare spell on the house. . . .'[22] Unstinted praise was also showered on Ranu Adhikary for her performance as Aparna in another show. The language used to praise Ranu in *The Englishman* as using her 'deft art to elevate the Bengali stage, in sooth, the Bengali nation' is indicative of how in three decades, Bengali society has accepted with grace the presence and participation of women from respectable families in theatre, at least under the auspices of the Tagore family.

The story of the public theatre was of course different. Here, Rabindranath's plays had to compete with those of the reigning emperors of theatre of the time and also fight for the attention and patience of the audience which were both notoriously fickle. Another important fact was that Rabindranath was never directly associated with the public stage which is why whether or not his plays would be staged depended on the taste and whims of the director or manager. It was also connected to the Box Office and only when a play was accepted by the audience could it have a long run. The other interesting point is that the works of Rabindranath which were performed in the theatre were not just his dramas. His novels and short stories were dramatized for the stage at various times. Sometimes the performance of his plays got caught up in the power struggle going on behind stage and sometimes his plays were used as a last resort to win the attention of the audience. Finally, it was the actresses who were the focus of attention in Tagore plays for two reasons—first, it struck everyone that Tagore's plays were far more sophisticated and subtle compared to the ones normally running in the theatres and the interpretation of his female roles by the uneducated and unsophisticated actresses of the time was something worth watching. Second, the songs of Rabindranath (*Robibabur Gaan*) was also quite different from the either the classical-based songs (kalowati) performed by the professional singers as well as the popular songs of the stage. Yet songs were central to the performances. As far as the plays performed in the public theatre are concerned, I have identified two phases—the first phase where Rabindranath was not even remotely connected with the performances and the latter stage in the 1920s when he and other members of his family were.

As early as 1886, two plays of Rabindranath were running in Calcutta's public theatres. *Kyatir Birambana* was performed on 6 April at Emerald Theatre with Ardhendu Sekhar Mustafi in the lead role and there were five performances. But far more popular was Rabindranath's novel *Bou Thakuranir Haat* which was dramatized as *Raja Basanta Roy* by Kedar Nath Chowdhury. On 3 July 1886, it was first performed at the Great National Theatre. When the theatre was auctioned off, the actors of the Great National Theatre formed the Great National Theatre Company and performed the play at the Opera House on Lindsay Street on 29 August and 11 September 1886. The same company under the name of the National Theatre Company performed at the same hall on 18 September and on 16 October at the Howrah Town Hall. On 23 October 1887 it was performed for the first time at the Emerald Theatre and then performed again there many times. In this play, Bonobeharini or Bhuni showed her calibre.[23] The play was stopped by Girish Ghosh in Emerald when he became manager on 11 November 1887.[24] When Girish Ghosh left Emerald for Star, its performance started again from 7 April 1889 and there were six performances in 1890, eleven in 1891, two in 1892, one in 1894, and nine in 1895. The play was revived in Minerva where again it went through changes in name and fortune due to Girish Ghosh's intervention. In Minerva, the first performance was on 6 April 1901. The advertisement in *Bengalee* said:

> Minerva Theatre Saturday, 6 April at 9 p.m. / the first splendid representation of Babu Rabindranath Tagore's historical / Tragedy / Raja Basanta Ray / Dramatised by Late Kedarnath Roy Chowdhury / Full of Pathetic situations / Thrilling decapitation of grey haired uncle Raja Basanta Ray by Maharaja Pratapaditya / scenery and Costumes as usual in the Minerva / Bright-Brilliant-Original and Interesting / Come and see and then pass your honest opinion. N. Sircar Manager

There were nine performances in 1901. The thirteenth performance on 25 June 1902 was a special performance in honour of the Coronation of Emperor Edward VII. There were five performances in that year. In 1903, Girish Ghosh was brought to Minerva as Manager in December and on 10 January 1903, the name of the play was changed to *Pratapaditya*. And as the advertisement said in Bengalee on 9 January 1904:

Sunday at candle light / The foremost poet of Bengal, Rabindranath's *Pratapaditya* / Look to the other side of the shield / Look how the master mind delineated the boistered up Bengali Hero / Refresh your memory regarding old tales . . .

It is quite possible Girish was in favour of totally stopping the play but he could not stop the performance of the play when Amarendranath Dutta was present.[25] Around this time, Kshirode Prasad Bidyabinode's *Pratapaditya* was being performed in Star and there is no indication that Rabindranath's plays were performed in Star during this phase. In Minerva in 1904 there were nine performances of *Pratapaditya* and then suddenly Kshirode Prasad's *Pratapaditya* starts and Rabindranath's *Pratapaditya* or *Raja Basanta Ray* ends after the fifteenth performance. It is possible that this had something to do with the fact that Amarendranath, who was the leaseholder of Minerva, incurred huge debts from Monomohon Panday and so Amarendranath transferred the lease to Panday.

From 9 April, Rabindranath's *Raja O Rani* had started repeat performance at Minerva. Its first performance had already started at the Emerald Theatre on 7 June 1890 and then performed eighteen times in that year, ten times in 1891, five times in 1892, twice in 1893. It was a bold step for Motilal Sur and Mohendralal Bose to take when Tagore's *Raja O Rani* was started in Emerald, in which Gulfan Hori acted in the role of Sumitra which Gyanadanandini Debi had already made popular. In fact, this led to Abanindranath alleging that Gulfan was one of the 'youths' who had gatecrashed a performance at Jorasanko and copied Gyanadanandini's style. But it was an amazing feat in itself if she had been able to imitate the regal air of the lady of the leading family of the city by watching her perform once. Sisir Kumar Bose wrote in his *Eksho Bochhorer Bangla Theatre* that the performances in the play were so good that once again people thronged the doors of Emerald after a long time and past-ill repute was buried.[26] In the same year on 18 January 1893 it was performed at the Royal Bengal Theatre. In 1897, on the Emerald stage, the fame of the performance of *Raja O Rani* of 24 July spread so much that for the 11 September performance, the Maharaja of Natore and Rabindranath came to watch. Kshetramoni was outstanding as Mangala. In Minerva there were five performances of *Raja O Rani* in 1904. In 1905 the stage was swamped by Girish Ghosh's *Balidan* and *Sirajuddaula* and Dwijendralal Roy's *Rana Pratap*. There was no performance of Rabindranath's *Pratapaditya* under any name and there was only one performance of *Raja O Rani*. There were no more performances in Minerva between 1905 and 1909.

Amarendranath Dutt opened Classic with Girish Ghosh as Manager/Director and for the first three years plays by Rabindranath was performed there. In October, Girish Ghosh left Classic for non-payment of dues and took with him the manuscripts of two of his plays. In desperation, Amarendranath turned to popular novel of Rabindranath, *Chokher Bali* to salvage the depleted fortunes of Classic; for the role of Binodini he had Kusumkumari, his loyal heroine, in mind. He had asked Girish Ghosh to dramatize it but Girish refused saying that he would not touch such an immoral play and he would not let such a degenerate play be performed in any theatre he was associated with. Girish Ghosh's antagonism to Rabindranath may have been social prejudice or professional jealousy but he is also consistent in his argument that it was up to theatre-lovers like him and others to make performance in 'improving' plays the means to reform and save the fallen women who came to the theatre under his protection.[27] Anyhow, once Girish left, Amarendranath started with *Chokher Bali*. But despite the fact that the book was a hit running into the second edition, despite the great performances, despite the varied strategy he used like distributing gifts, use of attractive sets in the Parsi theatre style, the play did not run.[28] Jagattarini had performed well as Annapurna along with great performances by Kusumkumari, Pannarani and Harisundari (Blackie). It ran only for four days. Amarendranath also dramatized other works of Rabindranath despite arguments from many that the poet's works were not suitable for the public theatre. Amarendranath was always an adventurer and he also dramatized Dalia as *Jibone Morone* in which he created two characters, Taher and Rangila. In this play he cast Sushilabala (Bengal's nightingale) as Taher and Charubala as Rangila. There was a great rush for tickets for the 1911 performances and *Bangabasi* praised the overall production and acting and singing. It added that Sushilabala's acting was so good that it was doubtful whether any man would be able to match that.[29] In Star in 1913–14, two other stories of Rabindranath were dramatized—*Shaasti* as *Abhimaanini* where Kusumkumari starred as Chandari and *Didi* as *Akalanka Shashi* where Kusumkumari was Shashi, Tarasundari was Basantakumari and Subasini was Mrinalini. Amarendranath and Kusumkumari having returned to Star acted in both the plays—Kusum as Chandara in *Abhimanini*, Sumitra in *Raja O Rani* and Binodini in *Akalanka Shashi*.

Another play that ran for many days was *Raja O Rani*. The first performances in the different theatres were 7 June 1890 at Emerald, 18 January 1893 at Bengal, 24 July 1897 at its Classic Theatre is Emerald stage, 20 March 1910 at Kohinoor, 18 May 1912 at Star, 20 November 1912 at the Monomohon Theatre and 29 August 1923 at the Art Theatre on the Star stage. In 1912, after the death of Girish Ghosh, Amarendranath was at Star's helm. In *Raja O Rani* he cast Sushilabala as Sumitra, in which role she excelled. Because of her musical talent, she also sang the songs of Ela's friends (sakhi) (*Bajibe sakhi banshi bajibe or sakhi oi bujhi banshi baje*).

The second phase, where a subtle change occurs, takes place in the 1920s and 1930s. In this phase Rabindranath actively participated in theatre where along with the older plays, *Shesh Raksha* was dramatized by Rabindranath at Sisir Bhaduri's request. *Baikunther Khata* was performed by the Art Theatre, Monomonhon Natyamandir, and Natyaniketan in 1932–4, *Bashikoron* was performed at the Art Theatre together with *Grihaprabesh* and *Chirakumar Sabha* was performed under Ahindra Chowdhury's direction with Rabindranath's support and help from Gaganendranath and Dinendranath Tagore. In all the plays performed in this period the actresses were able to successfully perform and sing according to the style prescribed by Rabindranath and Dinendranath Tagore. Most of the plays in this phase were also dramatized and edited by the author himself. Like in *Grihapravesh* which was to be performed by the Art Theatre, he made the end explicit so as not to add to any confusion in the mind of the audience and also added a new character Baishnabi who explains the story through songs. He also added songs to make them more attractive to the audience.[30] Niharbala specially has been singled out many times for her outstanding performance in *Raja O Rani* as Nirbala[31] though a letter to the Editor in *Nachghar* criticized her for her laughable mannerisms.[32] Another important aspect of Rabindranath's plays was the songs and the actresses' performance was closely connected to their ability to sing. This is evident from the announcement that the Art Theatre secured the services in 1925 of Indubala and Kanak who were as good as Ashcharjjyamoyee and Angurbala in singing.[33]

Ashcharjjyamoyee though a Nepali was so popular for her singing in Bengali Theatre that in the advertisement, though she had a small role as a sakhi, it was written that 'Those three famous songs *Jodi se*, etc., will be sung by Ashcharjjamoyee, the nightingale of our stage.'[34] It further wrote that the mistakes of Niharbala that had been noticed in her role of Nirbala in *Raja O Rani* seems to have disappeared in her performance as Himu in *Grihaprabesh*. She not only sang well but was also perfectly true to the *Rabindrik* tradition. Initially, the audience, used to Niharbala's histrionics in other plays, was becoming restive but when she started singing the sad song *oi moroner sagar pare chupi chupi* the 'barbaric' audience became quiet and docile just like a tamed snake and till the last screen dropped no one uttered another word. Sushilasundari's performance as Mashi was perfect and though the Editor of *Nachghar* had been apprehensive as to whether anyone other than Tarasundari would have been able to perform the role but Sushilasundari managed to surprise all.[35] But despite all these rave reviews, within a few months its performance was stopped because it was no longer popular and empty seats greeted the performances. *Nachghar* called it a great shame and misfortune for the nation.[36] In the same journal, an important point was raised in a letter to the editor where the writer, a Sachin Sen of Gariahat Lane says that 'there is always fear in the audience that like in the past, actresses might misinterpret Rabibabu's songs and play with the notes but not capture the essence. That will be the unkindest cut of all'. The critic feels that those 'who have become used to watching plays under Rabindranath's own direction have become dazzled by them and . . . the staging of *Grihapravesh* in the Art Theatre is a tragedy of high intention, self defeated'.[37]

Hemendra Kumar Roy in his editorials stressed that it is very important that the uneducated actresses understand the meaning of Rabibabu's songs and not just pick up the tune. There must be stress on his rhythmic arrangement, resonance, imagery and sentiment. Just because one is an expert singer does not mean that he or she will be able to sing Rabindra Sangeet. He refers to a famous singer who tried for fifteen days to learn *mama jouban nikunje gaahe pakhi* then left in shame. Among the singers, according to Hemendra Kumar Roy, Niharbala, though not so famous for her singing, managed to perform the songs best. Roy feels that the classical singers lose the emotive quality in their voices since they concentrate on the play of notes and are not able to perform Rabindranath's songs to perfection. His conclusion is that the classical singers consider themselves so great and Rabindranath's songs so beneath their dignity that they cannot please the audience.[38]

That the audience of Rabindranath's plays consisted of a large segment of women is obvious since one edition of *Nachghar* has dedicated a set of do's and don'ts for a feminine audience. Among the many points raised, they appeal to the women to keep young children accompanying them under control so that their crying does not affect the performance. *Nachghar* says that the mothers should bring enough supply of milk and other pacifiers so that the children stay quiet and that they should also refrain from loud conversations with their maid servants while ordering refreshments like tea, paan, soda, lemonade and snacks.[39]

Music in the plays of both Dwijendralal and Rabindranath played a crucial role and yet it led to certain distortions in tune and rendering which became permanent in the case of Dwijendralal, but gradually vanished in the case of Rabindranath for different reasons. In the case of Dwijendralal, the style of singing his famous song 'Ghana Tamashabrita ambar dharani' in *Chandragupta*, 'Amra emni eshe bheshe jayi' in *Nurjahan*, 'esho pran shokha esho prane' in *Durgadas* and 'E jibone purilo na shadh bhalobashi' in *Shah Jahan* have survived in two styles or gharanas. Those who have inherited the singing style of the actresses of the public theatre sing them quite differently from the way Dwijendralal Roy himself or his son Dilip Roy trained their students to sing.[40] On the other hand, there are some songs which were hardly sung outside the theatre and now have vanished since they were not preserved with notations by Dilip Roy or because while they were suitable in the context of the play, they were not suitable to be sung on their own. This is true of many of the songs of the farces. Some songs in written drama mention of the raga and taala in which they are to be sung and the public stage actresses trained in Hindustani classical music must have excelled in them (for example, 'Bandhi joto mon' in Bhimpalasri in madhyalaya sung by Meherunnissa in *Rana Pratap*).

In Rabindranath's plays, the difference is very evidentt since there have survived some recordings of Rabibabur gaan from before 1920. Krishnabhamini singing 'O je mane na mana' recorded in 1915, Purnakumari Dasi singing 'Ami chini go chini' recorded in 1905, Manadasundari Dasi singing 'Majhe majhe tobo dekha pai' and Ashcharjjyamoyee Dasi singing 'Oi bujhi banshi baje' recorded in 1921, show how differently the songs were sung and interpreted. Not only, the tune but the style of singing was totally different from the way Dinendranath Tagore taught from the mid-1920s. If one contrasts these with Niharbala rendering 'Ebar ujar kore' recorded in 1925 one can see the difference.[41] Unlike in Dwijendralal Roy's songs, where both styles survived the style of singing, Rabibabur gaan prior to Dinu Tagore's training in the theatre no longer exists thanks to the influential homogenizing mission of Visva-Bharati.

One may wonder why I have tried to study the performances of these writers/poets plays in the public theatre. Even if the case of Dwijendralal is understandable since his popularity was enhanced by the popularity that his plays have retained through performances in the public theatre over the ages, the same is not true of Rabindranath's plays. They were much more successful outside the public theatre. After all, the great poet himself tried to argue against the case. He never directly connected himself with theatre since as he did not believe that the greatest test of a drama is its performability. He wrote in 'Rangamancha' published in the journal *Nachghar* that he did not want his dramas to lose their independence and that it is only an appreciative reader who should be the soulmate of a drama like the love of a devoted couple.[42] There are differences of opinion in the editorials and the essays in *Nachghar* on this issue. While some like Nalini Mohon Roychowdhury,[43] one of the editors, considered it a pity that despite their brilliance *Raja O Rani* or *Bisarjan* or *Chokher Bali* could not fill the coffers of the theatre and that it was high time that the theatre-owners gave priority to artistic taste over financial gain, Promode Ranjan Dasgupta in an article 'Natyamanche Nabajug' thought it was educated actors like Sisir Bhaduri who made it possible for Rabindranath's plays to be successfully performed here.[44] On the other hand, Hemendra Kumar Roy, another Editor of *Nachghar*, believed that Rabindranath's plays should not be performed in public theatre—these plays, he felt, would not lift the theatre to a great height, they will fall down themselves. Only 'light' plays should be attempted and until the idealistic temper of the theatre is raised Rabindranath's plays should not be performed.[45]

No matter the debate, the fact remains that in our admiration we tend to study Rabindranath's works and songs in a vacuum. But it is undeniable that Rabindranath Tagore existed in a certain time and space and interacted with it. His works were not designated for any particular audience since they were available to all. In his lifetime, his works were open to interpretation by all—his plays were performed, songs sung in ways which he possibly never imagined but could not prevent. Therefore, for any researcher, these accounts are of as much importance as the interpretation that the producer of the work desired.

The women who were the inspiration of the poet's creation, those who read and interpreted them from his point of view as well as those who interpreted them in total opposition—are all important since any great writer's works belongs to the people.

Notes

1. Deb Kumar Roychowdhury, *Dwijendralal* (*Life*), Calcutta: Adhyan, 1964, p. 293.
2. Quoted by his biographer Deb Kumar Roychowdhury, op. cit., p. 300.
3. Aparesh Chandra Mukhopadhyay, *Rangalaye Trish Bachhar*, Calcutta: Granthan Publishers, 1972, p. 59.
4. Quoted in Sankar Bhattacharya, *Bangla Rangalaye Itihaser Upadan* (*1901–1909*), Calcutta: Pashchim Banga Natya Academy, 1994, p. 57.
5. Aparesh Chandra Mukhopadhyay, op. cit., pp. 40–1.
6. Dwijendralal Roy, *Amar Natya Jiibaner Arambha*, *Dwijendra Racanabali*, ed. Rathindranath Roy, Calcutta: Sahitya Samsad, vol. 1, pp. 708–10.
7. Shankar Bhattacharya, op. cit., p. 181.
8. Aparesh Chandra Mukhopadhyay, op. cit., pp. 60–1.
9. Shankar Bhattacharya, op. cit., p. 222.
10. Ibid., p. 236.
11. List of songs in Dwijendralal Roy's plays in Sudhir Chakraborty, *Dwijendralal Roy: Smaran Bismaran,* Calcutta: Pustak Bipani, Appendix 2, pp. 171–6.
12. Shankar Bhattacharya, op. cit., p. 242.
13. Ibid., p. 245.
14. Dwijendralal Roy, *Dwijendra Racanabali*, vol. I, op. cit., Intro, p. xxxi.
15. Shankar Bhattacharya, op. cit., p. 266.
16. Ibid., p. 291.
17. Ibid.
18. Dwijendralal Roy, *Dwijendra Rachanavali*, vol. I, op. cit., pp. 710–12.
19. Rudra Prasad Chakraborty, *Rangamancha o Rabindranath: Samakalin Protikriya*, Kolkata: Ananda Pub Pvt Ltd, 1995, introduction.
20. Amit Maitra, *Rangalaye Banganati*, Kolkata: Ananda Pub Pvt Ltd, 2004, p. 14.
21. *Indian Daily News*, 25 August 1923, quoted in Rudra Prasad Chakraborty, *Rangamancha O Rabindranath: Samakalin Protikriya*, op. cit., p. 60.
22. Ibid., p. 62.
23. Amit Maitra, op. cit., p. 107.
24. Shankar Bhattacharya, *Bangla Rangalaye Itihasher Upadan 1901–9*, Calcutta: Pashchim Banga Natya Academy, 1994, p. 145.
25. Shankar Bhattacharya, op. cit., p. 146.

26. Amit Maitra, *Rangalaye Banganati*, op. cit., p. 139.
27. *Girish Racanabali*, vol. V, ed. Debipada Bhattacharya, Calcutta: Sahitya Samsad, 2nd edn., 1991 pp. 364–5.
28. Ramapati Datta, p. 266.
29. *Bangabasi*, 6th Sravan, 1318 BS.
30. *Nachghar*, 18th Agrahayan, 28th samkhya, 1332 BS.
31. *Nachghar*, 8th Sravan, 12th samkhya, 1332 BS.
32. *Nachghar*, 15th Sravan, 13th samkhya, 1332 BS.
33. *Nachghar*, 5th Bhadra, 16th samkhya, 1332 BS.
34. Quoted in Amit Maitra, *Rangalaye Banganati*, op. cit., p. 32.
35. *Nachghar*, 25th Agrahayan, 29th samkhya, 1332 BS.
36. *Nachghar*, 15th Magh, 33rd samkhya 1332 BS.
37. Ibid.
38. *Nachghar*, 16th Asad, 6th samkhya, 1334 BS.
39. *Nachghar*, 22nd Magh, 34th samkhya, 1332 BS.
40. I owe this viewpoint to the famous exponent of Dwijendrasangeet, Krishna Chattopadhyay who received training from Dilip Roy.
41. See CDs one and two of the Rabi Pronam—Rabindra Sangeeter dhara 1904–2009, the 150th Birth Anniversary Commemorative Album (a ten CD collection), Kolkata: Saregama, 2010.
42. *Nachghar*, 2nd Aswin, 20th samkhya, 1332 BS.
43. *Nachghar*, 5th Asad, 7th samkhya 1332 BS.
44. *Nachghar*, 28th Falgun, 39th samkhya, 1332 BS.
45. *Nachghar*, 16th Asad, 6th samkhya, 1334 BS.

4

THE ACTRESS AND HER AUDIENCE

IT IS SAID that beauty lies in the eyes of the beholder. For the visual and performing art, this is undeniably true. No matter how well a play is written, its success is ultimately judged by the response of the audience. Thus, the importance of the audience cannot be over-estimated in any critical study of the theatre. It is, however, also a very difficult task because the audience does not normally leave any record of its reaction. When the study is of theatre in the past, the task is not only difficult but also daunting. A researcher has to depend only on newspaper or journal reports and the memory of the people concerned. Sometimes its reflection is seen in contemporary literature. It is from all these sources that I have tried to visualize the audience of early twentieth century in Calcutta—the public who visited the professional theatres of Calcutta between 1900 and 1930—a time when the theatre wove its magic over the cosmopolitan society of Calcutta before cinema cast its mesmerizing bait.

The relationship between drama and the audience has since time immemorial been interactive. However, with the establishment of private and professional theatres there was the beginning of a separation of the fictional stage world and the audience. Admission prices limited the social composition of the audience and with it came the beginning of the passivity of the audience and the emergence of a code of behaviour. The theatre design of stalls replacing pits ensured sedate behaviour and footlights became the literal barrier which separated the audience and the stage.[1]

But the involvement of the audience both during and outside the performance remained constant. Their influence was present in the pre-production—writing of the drama, casting, advertisement, during production—acting styles, introduction of music and dance and post-production in the critical appraisal of the viewers. Economically, the theatre is tied to a willing audience which pays to watch the performance and the sponsors and patrons of theatre. Any new directions in the shape of both new playwriting and new performance objectives/techniques depend precisely on that audience.[2]

This audience was so varied. There were those who considered the theatre to be evil and who tried their best to prevent impressionable members of their family and their friends from falling prey to its magic. There were others who could not resist the lure of the theatre and wanted to be a part of the tinsel world. Monomohon Goswami in an essay, 'Why I love the theatre' recalls the surprise and distress of his family members and friends when, on completion of his university studies and passing the law degree, he spurned his lucrative job as a deputy and indulged in his love for theatre. They could not understand why a young healthy youth should spoil his life and health staying up nights to watch theatrical performances.[3] This can be understood if we read the description of what the audience of the theatre in the early days had to bear. In his essay 'Sekaler Theatre', Hemendra Kumar provides a picture of the three-tier seats of the ordinary audience—stalls of bentwood chairs priced at Rs. 2, the pit with benches with back rest at Re. 1 and the gallery below the royal boxes which was only a 'slight improvement on a bird's perch' at 8 *annas*. The audience had to fan themselves to survive the intense heat by buying hand-fans and since there were no seat numbers, reserving a seat also needed dexterity and muscle-power. Often, the performances lasted from dusk to dawn and attending one performance required at least a couple of days of recuperation.[4]

Some were so irresistibly drawn to theatre that they were willing to forsake fortune, family, and friends or even brave social ostracism for it. The case study of Amarendranath Datta more or less encompasses all these. The tradition of watching performances was prevalent in almost all Bengali families and from his childhood Amarendranath watched Jatra and dramas on his father's lap. With the onset of youth, he secretly became a regular at the public theatres and soon abandoned his studies to join the theatrical groups as an actor. Soon, his contact with the theatre became a bone of contention with his family members and he left his home and settled down with the members of the theatrical company in his garden-house. Though he became estranged from his family due to his passion for both acting as well as the leading actresses, his unflagging efforts to make the public theatres of Calcutta popular is undeniable. As an actor, singer, dramatist, editor of theatre journals, *Saurabh* (1895), *Rangalaya* (1901), *Natyamandir* (1910), *Theatre* (1914), he was unsurpassed. His efforts to attract audiences included the use of the element of surprise and extravagance in the advertisements and distribution of free passes. He introduced changes in the production at the Classic Theatre by distributing advertisement posters, handbills and placards, innovating the backdrops, costume, theatricals props, acting styles and introducing singing and dancing. One interesting innovation to attract the public was that instead of the prevalent poster paper, Amarendranath used ivory-finish paper and printed them in different colours.[5] Amarendranath was in fact creating only a diversion for the audience, but this sensationalism only partially satisfied them visually without stimulating their intellect. His over-realistic attempts on stage could not hold any audience for long because it was reducing theatrical realism to absurdity. Finally, as a critic points out, lack of discipline in his personal habits and in his management made sure that 'for all his rebellious enthusiasm for the new' he could not keep his audience in his grip.[6]

There were some who were appreciative of the theatre as an art but who abhorred the company of the artists especially the 'fallen' actresses. Amarendranath's elder brother Dhirendranath was a typical example. He too was a theatre buff and was approached by Girish Ghosh to build a theatre but he was so disgusted by the 'drunken behaviour of the actresses at Star Theatre' that he refused to be associated with theatricals.[7]

There were very mixed feelings about the theatre. Many different shades were highlighted in the various views expressed and the only consensus was that there was no consensus. As compared to the spate of writings condemning the theatre as a den of vices, a change of heart occurred gradually for many. I will compare two occasions, one in 1879 and the other in 1912. In the first, a meeting was held in Dhaka when The National Theatrical Company went to perform there. A campaign was launched against schoolboys watching performances by actresses on the threat of dismissal from schools.[8] Within a few decades, the tone had changed. Bhupendranath Bose, during the Memorial Service for Girish Ghosh in the Town Hall on 6 September 1912 said that 'twenty years ago, men of culture and refinement used to shun the Bengali stage as an undesirable place but with its gradual improvement in all respects it was now a *useful* (emphasis mine) institution of the country and enjoyed the sympathy of the educated men'. The change was unmistakable. The gentlemen connected with the stage were no longer looked down upon.[9] As Hemendranath Dasgupta said in 1944, the importance of drama could never be overestimated. According to him, the national movements would have proved to be short-lived had it not been for the dramas produced at the time. 'At the time of the greatest need the dramas acted like a great inspiration and changed the servile mentality of the people. In fact at the time of the Swadeshi movement what hundred lectures could not do was accomplished by one single performance of *Sirajudaula* or *Mir Kasim*.'[10]

The fortunes of the different theatres also depended on the popularity of the plays. The fight over increasing the number at the Box Office took different forms. This was closely connected to the competition between the different theatres. There were attempts to sabotage performances by the contestants in various ways. Hemendranath Dasgupta relates how Amarendranath tried to destroy Girish Ghosh and Minerva's reputation through the use of placards and cartoons showing Girish Ghosh as an aging actor going down in the weighing scale compared to Amarendranath of Classic.[11] At other times, the managers and director/actors were inspired to try out new innovations to win over the hearts of the audience—sometimes adopting a new style and sometimes a new writer. When dramatic adaptations of Bankim Chandra's novels were made the rage by the Bengal Theatre and in *Durgesnandini*, Sarat Chandra appeared as Jagat Singha on horseback on stage. The play was such a huge success that Girish Ghosh duplicated it at the National Theatre but he underestimated the expectation of the audience because even his acting prowess could not make up for the lack of the presence of the hero on horseback on stage.

When theatre was started, performances were held on Saturdays alone but gradually Wednesday performances were started because on Saturday, the office 'babus' left for their home, in the village. When Avinash Kar, manager of national experimented with a Sunday 2 p.m. performance, it met with a resounding success. Henceforth, performances were held thrice a week including Sundays and then candlelight and matinee shows on special occasions were started.

Different kinds of bait were used to attract the public. Besides different kinds of gift items to attract the audience, particularly women, an advertisement in *Amrita Bazar Patrika* in 1905 referred to the offer that thousands of copies of Manomohon's dramas would be given away at half-price during a performance of his play. This was considered to be a real treat and the audience was asked to book seats early to avoid disappointment.[12]

Among the discerning audience were the critics who judged the performance, dress, sets and music. Their views are vividly expressed in articles in the leading journals on theatre. The audience as well as the producer was very conscious about the fact that the plays should be suitable to the prevailing taste. Sometimes plays were shortened, dialogues and actions changed, music increased or reduced according to the requirements and mood of the theatre-goer. After the 1927 performance of *Shahjahan*, a comment was made in *Nachghar* that the times had changed since Dwijendralal had written the play and it was necessary to make changes. The critics were often dissatisfied with the production of various plays, especially the costumes, backdrop, make up, etc. Manomohon Goswami in *Natyamandir*[13] claims that costumes were not changed according to the character so that unless one had a programme in his hand, one was never certain about who was performing each role. Only slight changes were made in the headgear and the hair of the leading characters. Both Ram and Jahangir wore the same costume. Even this slight adjustment was absent in the female characters. Sita and Nurjahan looked exactly the same. The extras suffered the worst fate. There was a fixed costume called the 'sakhi suit' with ruffles over the chest, and no matter which country, India, Persia, Turkey or Greece formed the background, the costume remained constant. The audience demanded ostentation more than accuracy in detail. Every hero appeared on stage dressed in the 'Highlander' style.

It was the Star Theatre which first became aware of the need to create costumes which would bring out the true qualities of every character in the dramas performed there. But these efforts were not always appreciated by the audience who preferred to be dazzled rather than be confronted with reality. So the majority of the performances continued the old system. The general trend of the producers was to concentrate not on the characters as portrayed by the writer but on the actor who was to play the role. If a lesser-known actor was to dress as emperor for a while, his dress would be old and ordinary but if the leading star was performing in a vital role as the emperor's subordinate, his costume would outshine that of the emperor in its splendour. No attention was paid to the time, lapse or suitability of occasion regarding dress. For example, the actor would hardly ever remove his sword before going to 'sleep' in the play.

Nachghar on 13th Agrahayan 1924 wrote that as Aurangzeb in *Shahjahan* Danibabu sported a peculiar dress. He wore an artificial black beard, a 'piran' or full coat up to his knees, white socks and shoes made of blue velvet with zari work. On his head he wore a red turban with a few strands of hair visible in the front. When he appeared on stage in this costume, it was always difficult for the audience to recognize him as Aurangzeb.

The facial makeup was highly unprofessional. There was often a clash of egos and 'images' of the actors and actresses with the requirements of the play and in most cases, the former triumphed. Prevailing fashions regarding hairstyles, eyebrows and lip-colouring also played an important role. 'Forward' wrote on 9 November 1924 that 'from behind the grey hair beard and moustaches the youth of the actor was bursting forth from his glowing cheeks, which in fact ought to have been shaded from below his cheekbones'—this was about Ahindra Chowdhury's *Shahjahan.*

In the advertisements, the audience lurks covertly. It is they that the advertisement is aimed at and therefore reflects their temper and opinions. The advertisements reveal a number of interesting trends. When a performance was heralded by an advertisement, certain phrases like *ananda samvad* (good news) or *chiranatun* (eternally new) feature regularly. Sometimes, before the date and venue was announced, an advertisement ploy was used where an appeal was created by the publication of the name of the play or the dramatist or the actors who were to perform. Besides announcing first performances and grand revivals, sometimes advertisement notices appeared when a show was extended due to the earnest request of the audience. For example,

> On special request of the audience / for one night only / the late Dwijendralal's greatest historical drama / to be performed at Star theatre / under the direction of the Art Theatre Ltd / on 10th Phalgun, Friday, at 7.30 P.M.

One advertisement for the Minerva Theatre for January-February 1931 said that 'Bhupen Babu's new sensational play *Desher Dak*—a play that educates and edifies' would be performed.[14]

There was a trend in the advertisements to announce the presence of famous personalities as chief guests at performances to attract the public. The advertisement in *Amrita Bazar* for the benefit night of Monomohon Roy announced that the performance would be 'under the distinguished patronage and immediate presence of Maharaj Kumar Shashi Kanta Acharya, Bahadur of Mymensingh'.[15]

A change is also noticeable in the content of the advertisements regarding the presence of singing and dancing girls. There are references to 'fancy drill of Amazons in Arms' in *Ronjaboti*,[16] 'fair artisans in holiday apparel, pretty sailor boys, girls in Japanese costume' in *Bahaba Batik* and gorgeous stage settings like in *Gairik Pataka*.

'Dramatic thrills, splendid acting, gorgeous settings, melodious music, delightful dances, soul stirring songs, costumes—a display of colour never exhibited before on Bengali stage.'[17]

With the sweep of the entertainment scene by the Talkies, the advertisements perhaps reflected this dominance. In the newspapers of the 1930s, for example, film advertisements cover almost the entire entertainment columns though a few theatres, Monomohon, Star or Minerva persevere with their advertisements, which however appear quite drab and small in comparison. Only occasionally are there flashes of flamboyance when there are special occasions like Doljatra, or a new performance or a new guest. In Minerva on 5 April 1930, an advertisement in *Advance* showed that 'in the immediate presence of the Hon'ble Chief Justice of Burma and the Hon'ble Justices of the Calcutta High Court and other high officials and advocates' a new performance was held.[18]

That the audience sometimes played a crucial role for a performance can be illustrated by an example from the 1930s when a proposed visit by the Minerva Theatre to Serajgunj, organized by the zamindar, Birendranath Roy, was stopped by an agitating public. The unique event was covered by three reports on 5 April, 10 April and 11 April in *Advance*. The correspondent at Serajgunj reported that the people there 'believe that in view of the grim struggle that the country has thrown itself it is not the time proper for indulging in such amusements as are positively calculated to dissipate the national energies. Specially this is the week of the Jallianwala Bagh massacre, when people all over the country become sorrowfully reminiscent of that tragedy. In consideration of all these things the people here are not in a mood to entertain the expensive luxury of Calcutta theatricals.' On 10 April, it was reported that a huge public meeting was held under the auspices of the Theatres' Boycotters Association in the maidan (field) near Elliot bridge condemning the proposed performances. Local school, national school headmasters and satyagrahis and others exhorted the gathering to support the resolution. The Association was threatened by the zamindar that he would bring a damage suit against Maulana Siraji, Maulana Basiruddin Muktar and Sj Sachindra Kr. Bose—the three signatories of the notice of boycott. The meeting ended at midnight. This was followed by a ban on meetings and processions by the renewal of Police Act 30, by the Police Superintendent of Pabna within the jurisdiction of the Serajgunj municipality. Finally, the drama ended through a small notice on 11 April which says that the Minerva Theatrical Company was prevented from visiting Serajgunj.

Every coin has its flip side. Often, the audience came under scrutiny from the other side of the stage as well. In 1927, Amritalal Basu, manager and dramatist, wrote in distress that despite the fact that the audience have been provided with the comfort of sofas and couches, they have, deteriorated in taste and quality. Previously, the audience had been comprised educated and well-dressed gentlemen whereas now they did not pay that respect to theatre.[19] Much earlier Rabindranath Tagore in 1902 had warned theatre to take the audience seriously, not to take their intelligence for granted and to allow space for the audience's imagination. There is no doubt that over a period of time, the audience had changed in its profile, in social and educational backgrounds, which ultimately determined its taste and demands. The theatre too, ever since it became economically dependent on the audience, has had to innovate and adapt to the audience. This is true of all public media but much more of theatre since the audience it faces is a live one and the responses immediate. No drama can run if it is not appreciated by the audience—no matter what its content or motive. In fact, the success and failure of a dramatic performance depends less on its content and quality and more on its acceptance by the audience. So in the ultimate analysis, the audience is in no small way responsible for the improvement or degeneration of the theatre. Also, no matter how alluring all the other entertainments in Calcutta in the first half of the twentieth century were, the charm of theatre survived through all its vicissitudes largely due to the loyalty of its audience. It is no mean credit that ultimately no one in Calcutta from the school-going teenager to the spiritual leader of the, age Sri Ramkrishna Paramhansa, was immune to the magic of the stage.

NOTES

1. Susan Bennett, *Theatre Audiences*, London: Routledge, 1990, pp. 3–4.
2. Ibid., p. 4.
3. Quoted in Debashis Majumdar and Sekhar Samaddar, eds., *Shatabdir Natyachinta*, Calcutta: A Mukherjee & Co., Pvt Ltd., 2000.
4. First published as editorial in *Nachghar*, quoted in Debashis Majumdar and Sekhar Samaddar, eds., *Shatabdir Natyachinta*, op. cit., pp. 196–8.
5. Ibid., p. 152.
6. Kironmoy Raha, *Bengali Theatre*, New Delhi: National Book Trust, 1978, p. 78.
7. Ibid., pp. 119–20.
8. Quoted in Hemendranath Dasgupta, *The Indian Stage*, vol. III, New Delhi: Munshiram Manoharlal, 2002, pp. 15–16.
9. Ibid., p. 82.
10. Hemendranath Dasgupta, op. cit., vol. III, p. 58.
11. Ibid., vol. IV, p. 13.
12. *Amrita Bazar Patrika*, 6 January 1905.
13. *Natyamandir*, 3rd year, Sravan, 1339 BS, 1932.
14. *Advance*, January–February 1931.
15. *Amrita Bazar Patrika*, 6 January 1905.
16. Ibid., 5 January 1905.
17. *Advance*, June 1930.
18. Ibid., 3 April 1930.
19. *Nachghar*, 23 Sravan, 1927.

5

CAUGHT BETWEEN TRADITION AND MODERNITY

It was only in 1872 that the doors opened to the public with the price of a ticket being the only restriction for entry to the hall of magic. Magical it certainly was, especially with women acting in female roles in 1873 once again after five decades. But magic was now not only a passion or worship or even a livelihood, but a profitable business venture. Thus, a theatre production meant not only putting together a group of like-minded and talented individuals with a play at hand, it meant finding a financier 'captain' and a stage on which fortunes would to be made or destroyed. The history of theatre in Calcutta is all too often studied as if from the point of view of the audience. The overwhelming majority of the discussions are on the subject of the plays and the performance, the style of acting, singing, dancing by the actors and actresses and then about the art of the dramatist. There is very little discussion about the activity behind the scenes. Theatre management and production is, in fact, a monumental and complex task. The managers, financiers, lease holders, patrons, etc., who actually form the backbone of a theatre production are numerous, but play very ambiguous roles. There is constant undercutting and ruthless competition by them as well as by the masters of the theatre groups so that a veritable web of intrigue unfolds. In this chapter, I intent to hold up only one small portion of that large kaleidoscope for perusal.

The theatre was always threatened by financial losses. The performance of a play involved a large expense, the largest part being the playhouse. Previously, the plays of the amateur theatre were performed in the houses of the well-to-do and the roles were performed by men of leisure who acted for pleasure and did not need to be paid. Also, the audience previously played no real decisive role. They were invited guests who were offered a fare which was rare entertainment and therefore there was no real accountability fixed on them. But everything changed when entertainment was provided in exchange for money. Gradually, ownership shifted from men of means who wanted entertainment, to men who wanted to make money out of entertainment. In order to keep the Box Office rolling, it became more and more necessary to create better and more attractive plays. Of course, it was not only the content that needed to be inspired but the form and outward show, including the advertisement which became more and more the cynosure of all eyes. With more than one theatre being established, the competition became cut-throat. All members of the theatre were caught in the maelstrom of necessary change, some more visible than others. The actresses had an additional accountability of loyalty to their mentors and lovers, not only to art or their employer. Caught between many a battle in this entire period of the public theatre, the actress hardly ever made a decision on her own.

Among the many battles being played out in the arena of the theatre backstage, I am going to discuss a battle between two giants who were not just actors but may be called path-breakers in the world of theatre. Again, it must be remembered that there are many reason why posterity remembers some and not others and the reason is not always only talent. Girish Ghosh became a colossus during his lifetime and for the actress he was like a large tree providing shelter and nourishment, having brought them into the harsh sunlight from within the dark and dank brothels. At times, this dependence by many actresses made him think that he was responsible for all aspects of their life and in most cases it was true. Like other actresses, Binodini believed that, though she suffered material and mental loss and trauma due to him, Girish was their sincere protector. Even posterity gives Girish's versatility recognition and respect and as is the way of the world, all those who go against an idol are inevitably punished by collective forgetfulness.

If in the first few three decades of public theatre Girish Ghosh's presence and contribution to the theatre is undeniable, then that is also true of Amarendranath Dutta whose innovations and ideas pumped in new blood to the moribund theatre of the 1920s. Even though Amarendranath was very close to Girish and in fact worked closely with him when Classic brought in Girish as manager, it was inevitable that Girish would find his new-fangled ideas unacceptable and most critics were of the same opinion. As the two paths crossed, clashes were inevitable. What I find interesting is that the newer path would never have been possible if the way had not been shown by the older one and yet the new path was necessary if Bengali theatre had to move on to the next generation. It was seen as a declaration of defiance by a new philosophy, outlook, and enterprise but it must be admitted it was endorsed by the theatre-goers if not the critics. I would like to explore the war where youth with all its confident brashness clashed with the established traditions of theatre and its established giants.

Amarendranath Dutt (1876–1916), was bitten by the acting bug fairly early in his youth and despite all attempts by the 'reputed and respectable family' to which he belonged to prevent him from entering the profession, Amarendranath was adamant. While his father was alive the restrictions still worked but soon after his father's death, Amarendranath's brothers were unable to stop him from spending his time and finances on theatre. His studies soon ended and in a final desperate bid to turn his mind away from the 'despicable profession' Amarendranath's brothers involved him in the family business and arranged for the sixteen year-old to have a fourteen year-old bride, Hemnalini, as a steadying influence. The biography of Amarendranath Dutta by his elder brother Hirendranath's son Harindranath alias Ramapati Dutta,[1] is a very negative one and very much from the point of view of the family as the sufferer and Amarendranath the villain whose love for the theatre was seen as a facade for licentious living and obsession for the actress Tarasundari. Interestingly the account is more sympathetic in the description of Amarendranath's struggle in theatre as an artist and manager, possibly because the biographer, Harindranath, was himself involved with theatre and music from his childhood. Another autobiography by a contemporary actor and playwright, Aparesh Chandra Mukhopadhyay, contrary to expectations, analyses quite sympathetically the rise of Amarendranath despite the fact that Aparesh was always in an opposing group and had personal differences as well.[2] What emerges from the contemporary and later biographies and Amarendranath's writing in his own theatre journals, *Saurabh* and *Rangalay*, is the tortuous path to stardom and success. Amarendranath's path was full of struggles, financial and emotional. He considered no attachment more important than his love for theatre and his determination to make a contribution to it. What is typical of the myopic race to which he belonged is that generations of theatre-lovers and critics have more or less ignored his contribution, possibly because he dared to be different. Especially in confronting the traditions of his age and the icon of Bengali theatre.

The first confrontation that Amarendranath had was with his family and an inherited duty to preserve the family prestige—he repudiated both. He felt no inhibition in either leaving his ancestral home and making the family garden-house into a retreat for actors and actresses, a veritable 'den of vices' according to his family members, or in demanding his share of the property without ascertaining its feasibility, or in summarily dismissing his duty to his wife and despatching her to her maternal home along with his son. The only person whom he was unhappy to disappoint was his mother and this is evident from the numerous letters referred to in his biography, but he felt he had no alternative.

There occurred then the much greater confrontation with the world of established theatre, a veritable war with other groups and the idol of the theatrical world, Girish Ghosh. It was for Amarendranath a momentous shock. Even if he knew that a break with his family and kin was inevitable because of the stigma attached to the profession he was about to embrace, it is doubtful if Amarendranath ever imagined that he would ever come to a clash with the great Girish Ghosh. It is necessary to bring out the whole relationship with Girish Ghosh not only to highlight the enormity of the task that Amarendranath set for himself when he tried to establish a new theatrical group but also to show the how two generations fought tooth-and-nail not only for art but for survival and finally to understand why generations of theatre-lovers and critics after Amarendranath have forsaken and ignored his contribution.

Girish Ghosh was not only a model for any aspiring actor, he was also a family friend. So it is not surprising that Amarendranath went to him for advice before starting a career as an actor. Girish apparently advised Amarendranath to become a patron of a theatre instead of an actor. Girish explained that as a son of a rich family he would not be able to bear the hardship of an actor's life.[3] The advice seemed very unreasonable to the twenty year old Amarendranath since he knew he did not have enough money to be a patron. He did not realise that Girish was implying using of the wealth of his family.

Though Girish Ghosh's contribution to and love for the theatre must be acknowledged, it cannot be denied that he was always on the lookout for a financier and had no compunction in using any means, fair or foul, to rope in a rich patron. The biography of Amarendranath reveals another twist in the story. It appears that Girish had been a close acquaintance of Amarendranath's eldest brother, Dhirendranath. On Girish's request Dhirendranath had promised to invest Rs. 30,000 in Girish's theatre but later appalled at the 'misdemeanor' in the theatrical circles, he went back on his word. Girish was very insulted and promised to take revenge by forcing at least one of Dhirendranath's family members to sink his money into theatre.[4] So Amarendranath's enthusiasm was providential. Though Amarendranath did not realize the dubious intent behind Girish's advice, he did bear the advice in mind and later tried his utmost to start a company and work towards removing the burdens of an actor's life.[5] Realizing that Girish would not help him to become an actor, Amarendranath decided to form his own theatre group. This task was not such a simple one. Every aspiring theatre group tried to get hold of a good stage along with a successful company, ranging from a financier, manager and playwright to actors and actresses. The first hurdle was finding a stage. For the twenty year-old Amarendranth, the unsuccessful fight over Bina Stage by three rival companies, one established and the other two fledgling, was an eye-opener.[6]

Amarendra Dutta and his troupe along with the secretary of the City Theatre, Nilmadhab Chakraborty, infiltrated into the Aparesh Chandra Mukhopadhyay group who had leased the Bina Theatre to form a theatrical company. This City Theatre also had the backing of Girish Ghosh and Nilmadhab wanted to rejuvenate his declining City Theatre and form the Gaiety Theatre. Taking advantage of the inability of Aparesh Mukherjee to pay the rent of Bina, Nilmadhab leased the Bina Theatre. Aparesh's group broke up, but unfortunately even Amarendranath could not get control of Bina. Finally, even Nilmadhab's Gaiety ran for only a few weeks. Amarendranath then re-formed the Indian Dramatic Club and leased the Emerald, Minerva, Bengal and Corinthian theatre stages and performed *Palashir Juddha, Bellik Bajar* and *Bishad* and won many accolades. Soon, Amarendranath realised that with his meagre resources without a permanent stage it would be impossible to continue with his group. A majority of the actors and actresses stayed at his garden-house and he fed and clothed them from the dwindling share of his inherited estate. His brothers who had been giving in to his financial demands were losing their patience. He, therefore decided to approach the rich Gopal Sil with the support of his friend Satishchandra Chattopadhyay. Gopal Sil's Emerald Theatre was closed at that point because the City Theatre which had been regrouped again at Emerald by Nilmadhab after the failure of Gaiety, also ran into trouble. Dwindling ticket sales led to financial losses and Gopal Sil decided to change his lessee. Amarendranath, at this opportune moment, tried to test his fortune. Gopal Sil was a close friend of his eldest brother but the deep affection that the financier had for his friend's brother made him reluctant to lease the theatre to Amarendranath. He 'could not let the young boy destroy his life by helping him enter a life of vice'.[7] He was however later persuaded through the intervention of a common friend, Shyam Madhab Roy.

Amarendranath may have changed his dream from becoming an actor to managing a theatrical company because he truly believed that he could improve the actor's lot financially as well as socially. He wrote that since the actor's sufferings in this country were celebrated and most people quite indifferent to improvement in the art of acting, he had taken up the task himself.[8] The greatest hurdle was the ignorance in the minds of people and this could be removed by communication. He started *Saurabh*, the first theatre journal in Bengali in 1895 in which articles, stories, plays, poems and notations of songs were contributed by all the leading actors and actresses of the day like Girish Ghosh, Binodini Dasi, Tarasundari Dasi, Narayani Dasi and Jadumoni Dasi. *Rangalay* was started later in 1901 and continued for four years. Panchkadi Bandopadhyay was its Editor and a number of well-known writers of Bengal of the time, Girish Chandra, Dwijendralal Roy and Kshirodeprasad, contributed to it.

Amarendra could not imagine a theatre without Girish's blessings. As he wrote in 1900, there was not a single actor in Bengal who had not been trained or influenced by Girish Ghosh. Three years before that, Amarendranath had approached Girish Ghosh to become the manager of his new Classic Theatrical Company but Girish Ghosh felt he could not join any group which was not yet established. Disappointed, Amarendranath inaugurated the Classic Theatre at the old Emerald theatre on Beadon Street with Girish's *Nala Damayanti* and the farce *Bellick Bazar*. The advertisement of the first show which came in his name as the lessee and manager said that the new theatre was opening with 'a medley of the cream of the staff of some of our Public Theatres, supplemented by infusion of new blood of Actors and Actresses of established reputation'. He added a note that 'owing to shortness of time, I have not been able to appear before the public with a New

Drama, as I fully intended to. I shall however do so soon. All that I now aspire to is to merit the sympathy of the public for appearing before them wthout waiting to be fully prepared for the honour.'[9]

Soon, Amarendranath realized that what he had actually inaugurated with the launching of a new company was a rivalry with the Girish-led Star Theatre. Within a few nights, Star's group with all the leading performers of the day started performing the same play *Haranidhi* under Girish's leadership and training. Though Classic's *Haranidhi* was praised, finding the sales of tickets dwindling, Amarendranath changed plays, chose the already popular *Debi Chaudhurani*, rewrote the script and added eleven songs. He changed the scenery, costumes and the audience were mesmerised at the realistic handling of dramatic scenes.[10] Despite everyone praising him for his acting, the sale of tickets was still disappointing. Not only was it demoralizing for the actors to act before an empty hall, but meeting regular expenses was becoming difficult.

There were many reasons why it was necessary for a theatre to concentrate on improving the financial aspect as well as the artistic one. Unlike the amateur theatre, which was funded by gentlemen with ample means, public theatre involved more men from the middle classes with a passion for theatre but without the means to indulge in it. So actors, directors, managers were all dependent on the theatre for their livelihood. Also, with theatre becoming professional these men had to belong to the theatre full-time and could hardly hold on to a primary profession and keep the theatre as a hobby. For the actress, of course, the same applied since most of them came from prostitute families which had no alternative source of income. Also I believe that once they joined theatre, continuing with their previous profession would be difficult since they were now the cynosure of all eyes and needed to maintain a certain aura of mystery as befitting a star. They could hardly be an ordinary prostitute servicing anyone anymore. Also, at least preserving an unstained reputation once they joined the stage was vital if the audience had to find them credible in their roles. The main objection evident in the newspapers in getting women from prostitute families as actresses in the roles of chaste women and divine goddesses or even in men with divine characteristics was that of unsuitability, as if they were in some way hoodwinking the public.

Even in the recent past, before theatre became public, actors and singers in the amateur theatres used to be given a pension or an honorarium by the local patrons. But with theatre moving away from the dependence circle of the patron, or the pensioner joining a theatre under a rival patron or even performing in plays which were considered unsuitable by the patron, resulted in abandonment by the patron. In such cases, the actor became dependent on his fellow theatre-folk to provide for his sustenance. The case of Ardhendu Sekhar Mustafi, the famous actor in the first era of the public theatre, is an example of the last. He was a pensioner of the Tagores of Pathuriaghata, and when he performed in a play *Kichhi Kichhu Bujhi* which satirized the Tagores, his pension was stopped.[11] He then became dependent on his co-actors like Amritalal Bose,[12] unlike Girish Ghosh who had a job as a clerk.

With the progress of theatre over a period of time, the novelty soon began to wear off and earnings correspondingly fell. The critics and the public now had reference points regarding the improvements and developments in world theatre through the numerous articles published in the journals of the time. It became evident by the twenties of the twentieth century that improvements in the sets and backdrops were essential to attract the audience and this competitiveness now motivated the different theatres to experiment with art work. All these experiments needed large financial resources and Amritalal Bose refers to placards which announced shows for the 'benefit of the stage' which was a means of acquiring funds to improve the stage sets.[13] Most of the time, these attempts to organise funds did not work and there were hundreds of cases going on in the different courts of Bengal and the capital city which pointed to the fact that the owners and managers were constantly going bankrupt. Also for the actress who had given up the profession that her mother led was now totally dependent on her salary from the theatre for livelihood and for their future.

Finally in the fifty years of public theatre that had passed, pure acting with songs and dances thrown in, had reached a saturation point. It was not enough to attract the audience any more. Dwijendralal, who being associated with the theatre, yet not in it, realized this and put it most aptly—the public wanted something 'new' all the time.

> *Notun kichhu koro, ekta notun kichhu koro . . . Ja hoy—ekta koro kichhu rokom notuntoro.*
>
> Do something new, do something new . . . no matter what—do *something* that is newer than before.
>
> (*Prayaschitta* perfomed as *Bahut Achha* in Classic)[14]

There has to be something new for people to explore every decade or so. The novelty of a woman on stage was wearing off. Now the Parsi theatre had brought in innovation which the purists may have looked down upon, but for an audience looking for thrills and entertainment it was something to look forward to. Amarendranath had caught the mood of the audience much more than his illustrious seniors and contemporaries.

While evaluating the two styles of management of Girish and Amarendranath, one is apt to take sides as most of the critics did. But instead of the fruitless mudslinging that the contemporary and later critics did, what is more useful now is to analyse what exactly the contribution of the two greats were. It is undeniable that Amarendranath's experiments would not have materialized at all if the base had not already been set by Girish over the past decades, but it is also true that fast-paced changes had become necessary, even though it continued to be denied by the established orthodoxy and rejected as frivolous, harmful and degenerate, or at least vulgar. This dichotomy has been the signature fight of the arts time and again and a familiar example is the crisis that the talkies wrought over the era of silent moving pictures.

It is to the credit of Girish that he was able to regularise the pay of the different grades of workers in the theatre. Managerial skills were his forte too—maintaining attendance registers and accounts of the income and expenditure revolutionised management in the National Theatre in 1877. This was when he was appointed manager with a fixed salary by Pratap Johuri who was the first non-theatre person to take over the ownership of the theatre with the motive of making it a successful business venture. Besides these innovations, Girish also started a trend which became a standard trend later, i.e., writing plays for the theatre. Interestingly, his practice which produced some of the most successful plays which till now are model plays, was looked down upon by the contemporaries and even later critics, who distinguished between playwrights writing plays to suit the taste of the less-educated and volatile audience and the dramatists who wrote from an inner compulsion. Girish, however, learned from the hard school of experience that the effort needed for the adaptation of popular novels and dramas was too great, especially since new plays had to be introduced regularly to retain the attention of the audience. It was simpler to write plays on already popular subjects to suit the needs of the stage, acting styles of the leading performers whom the audience were interested in watching and utilizing the talent available in the theatres.

Other innovations which became standard practice by the time Amarendranath came to the scene were revolutionary yet beneficial by any standard—the introduction of rehearsals, planning of stage sets and scenes, effective backdrop–changing with change of scenes, training of actors and actresses to produce the best performances, creating a new format and language for advertisements and organise overall stage management/direction. Even under Girish there were attempts to create surprises for the audience through the scenes of Durga Puja in *Ravana Badh*, creating theatre on stage in *Sitar Bibaha*, the play of clouds in the sky in *Abhimanyubadh* and the capture of Sita and Ravana's fight on the chariot through space in *Sitaharan*.[15]

The advertisements in the late nineteenth century, 1880s and 1890s refer to other stage tricks which aimed at keeping the audience awestruck and willing to visit the theatre repeatedly. The art director of Star, Jawaharlal Dhar, introduced unearthly sights through the use of lights. The advertisement for *Nala Damayanti* refers to a 'photo electric lotus' and *Kamale Kamini* to a 'mechanical golden bird', which flew on the stage. Finally, from almost the beginning, there was the lure of song-and-dance which brought people to the theatre. The use of songs in the modern style, and not classical, in theatre gave it legitimacy so that people could listen to all types of songs in the interest of the play though listening to it from a professional artist would be looked down upon.

Amarendranath learnt an important lesson that Box Office success was essential for any kind of improvement in art. He did not hesitate to take steps to address the problem. Unlike the established tradition in theatre of deserting a ship the moment it faced a threat, Amarendranath used shrewd management tactics which shook the old order and infused new life and vigour into the theatre world. He showed his genius for management by taking a number of new measures.

(a) Each performer would give 'free passes' at every performance to private friends to ensure that the hall was full. The objective was that these people would then spread the word of their good performance.

(b) He experimented with show timings. He started the Wednesday show in addition to the weekend. He introduced a new play on Saturday and once it was successful, he moved it to the Sunday show and started a new one. Finally on 2 February 1902, the Matinee show started with *Bhramar* at 2 p.m. Later, even 12 p.m. shows were started from 27 January 1903 and it was a measure of his success that all the shows ran to full houses.

(c) Frequent change of plays. Every time there was a reduction in sales of tickets, he would change the plays. Within five months, Classic performed ten plays. Shakespeare's *Hamlet* was translated into *Hariraj* by Nagendranath Chowdhury and was a hit. Still, Box Office success eluded him. He then thought of staging a musical and adapted Kshirodeprasad Vidya Binode's *Alibaba* and added songs. It is said that he took the play to Girish who made certain changes and composed the prelude.[16] In the end, his strategy paid rich dividends.

(d) Another of his innovations was in the field of advertisement. Instead of the staid and respectable language of the older theatre groups Star, Emerald, City, Minerva, Amarendranath used racy and dramatic language to arouse the interest of the audience. His handbills, unlike those in use before, began to use good quality ivory finish paper and coloured writing with attractive pictures of actors and actresses.[17] Not only were there long descriptions in the elaborate advertisements of the first and last scenes, there were often snide comments against his rivals who he claimed used songs simply as ploy to draw the audience. In one advertisement, taunts were also made regarding the previous immature dramatisation of great dramas. The audience were invited to come, learn how novels should be transformed into plays suitable for performance, not to arouse laughter in men, nor to excite low desires in young boys and not to humiliate the poet/writer by introducing irrelevant characters and unnecessary, vulgar songs.[18] Interestingly this advertisement where Amarendranath used the weapon of satire against rival theatres was when he had Girish Ghosh in his team in Classic as director. Already, he had embarked on his journey of flinging away discretion, seriousness and sentimentality which theatre had nurtured for so long in order to bring respectability.

(e) Aparesh also attributes Amarendranath's success to the audience. According to him, the audience who were so long forced to maintain a formal decorum at the other theatres were able to 'breathe a sigh of relief' at the freedom to 'pass comments, blow whistles, crack rude jokes' during the performances of Classic at Beadon Street. That was why when Classic ran to packed house, Star faced empty seats.'[19]

(f) Amarendra was able to lure away all the best stars from the various theatres to his Classic by giving them salaries eight times higher than what they received as well as providing them with bonuses of not less than Rs. 1,000 and other benefits. This created a sense of anticipation in the audience since this was unlike the other theatres where the same stars performed in all plays. In Classic, they were always surprised by new faces. In fact Amarendranath himself was a refreshing change from all the aging stars of the time, Girish, Mahendralal or Amritalal. 'He was', in the words of a dramatist of the time, Bhupendranath Bandyopadhyay, 'good looking, pleasant behaved with a melodious voice.'[20]

(g) In 1898 he used another ploy with great success—combining a film show (bioscope) with a play, *Alibaba*. The show at Bioscope was advertised in 1901 as 'series of superfine pictures from our world renowned plays' in order not to reduce the importance of the plays. His mythological flm *Shivratri* under the auspices of J.F.Madan and Co. was the first Bengali film.[21]

All these measures paid rich dividends and his plays *Alibaba* and *Bhramar* were unique cases in Bengali theatrical history for the sheer numbers in the audience. With *Bhramar* started a new era for backdrop and stage-props. Amarendranath as Govindalal in the play entered the stage on horseback and near—real sets had such a deep impact on the audience that at any time of the day there were 'house-full' signs at the counter. Amarendranath was crowned the *Beadon Streeter Keshari* (*Lion of Beadon Street*).

Amarendranath knew that despite his deep respect for the Natyaguru Girish, a clash was inevitable. Having refused to associate with Amarendra, Girish was now ranged against him at Star but by 1897, with *Alibaba* Classic had come of age. The Plague in 1898, saw the exodus of people from Calcutta, to safer areas. Sometime before, Girish, due to differences of opinion with Star authorities who dismissed his last two plays as products of a demented brain, had moved on. Taking advantage of the chaos that the Plague scare produced, Girish lured away some of the actors and actresses of Classic and formed a group which left town. Amarendranath was unfazed by the situation. He continued performances and organized relief work wholeheartedly with the help of his group members.

Then, hearing that Girish Ghosh was not attached anywhere, he invited him and his son Danibabu to join Classic. Girish joined in July 1898, and Amarendranath acted with the both of them in some successful productions. As the *Indian Mirror* said on 12 October 1898, 'the manager has been profuse in using his brains and purse in the getting up and mounting of the piece is a fact that would admit no denial.'[22] But in the meantime, with a change of lessee at Minerva, attempts were made to lure Girish away from Classic. Girish submitted and left Classic suddenly on 25 December 1898 after the first night of Amarendranath's new musical *Nirmala*. He however was unsuccessful in restoring life to the moribund Minerva and returned to Classic in March 1899. But this time Amarendranath was determined to be less lenient. The contract stipulated that Girish would write at least four plays a year for Classic of which at least two would be five-act plays.

After the unprecedented success of *Bhramar*, Girish Ghosh demanded from Amarendranath a share of Classic's profit since its fame was due to his presence. Girish claimed it would be for his own benefit since Girish would not leave Classic. But Amarendranath refused, saying that Girish had violated his contract by not providing a single new play to Classic and that all the successes of Classic were due to Amarendranath's own efforts. Besides, past experience proved that Girish would leave any theatre if he found better opportunities elsewhere. Girish was shocked at this refusal and stopped coming to the theatre. Amarendranath, hearing that Girish was again negotiating with Minerva, reminded him of his contract and offered to pay him a monthly salary at home if he would write plays for Classic. Realizing the depth of the injustice he had done to Classic by violating the contract, Girish, in five days, completed a play *Pandav Gaurab* and gave it to Amarendranath. But differences arose again when Amarendranath did not allow him to do the casting. Girish instructed Danibabu to leave Classic and join Star. When posters of the first performance of *Pandav Gaurab* in the presence of the Lt. Governor of Bengal, Sir John Woodburn, were distributed all around town, Girish, who was cast as

Kanchuki, left Classic for Minerva on 8 April 1900. Within a few days Girish also lured away Tinkadi Dasi who had become the lead in Classic after Tarasundari left. This time Amarendranath was furious and he brought an injunction against Girish since the contract mentioned that he had to provide four plays or pay Rs. 3,000. But technical difficulties made the injunction unsuccessful. A war of theatres began.

Amarendranath decided to pay Minerva in its own coin. When Minerva advertised a play he would immediately organise it in Classic and do it better—as in the case of *Sitara*. As the *Indian Mirror* commented on 19 July 1900, 'Babu Amarendra Nath Dutt is a firm believer in the maxim, 'whatever thy hand endeth to do, do it with all thy might'.'[23] Girish too used Amarendra's weapons to fight him. A handbill from Minerva said:

> Our representation, we feel bold to say, will prove to them that howling is not acting and that such a subject, at once serious and sublime ought not to be handled by quacks who will unscrupulously lay their hands on the most complicated cases without possessing the requisite qualification of even a common-place amateur.

Amarendranath replied in another handbill:

> We do not know—rather we are not ambitious of (*sic*) making a gigantic preface, but to appeal to our patrons and friends with due curtsey (*sic*) and dignity to come and see our performances and then compare! No doubt they will find a difference of Heaven and Hell! No more for the present! Now good bye!

The next day Girish wrote:

> N.B. It has been said that there is a difference of Heaven and Hell! Aye! Let us Hope so at least!

Amarendranath began to lampoon Girish through the handbills, transforming them into newspapers. Cartoons were published in which he showed in various ways that Classic was far better than Minerva, where Girish was. The most obvious one was the picture of a balance where Girish and Amarendranath were on either side and Amarendranath's side was shown as being heavier. Another cartoon was a tug-of-war contest in which Classic was able to overturn Girish's Minerva.

Finally, Amarendranath wrote a farce lampooning Girish and the Minerva Theatre. Whether it succeeding in hurting the sentiments of those it targeted or not, it did so well at the Box Office that Amarendranath admitted it brought in more money than all his other plays. In fact, all the other theatres suffered in this period. The Bengal Theatre soon shut down, Star could not pay its rent nor its actors and actresses and Minerva's leaseholder, Narendra Nath Sarkar, disappointed at Girish's failure against Classic, cancelled the agreement with Girish. Within a month, Girish again joined Classic on 24 November 1900. Whether in true humility or as a ploy, Amarendra announced his entry through a handbill which said that all the disputes with Girish, who was the true creator of all theatre and the trainer of all performers, had been his own fault. As a matter of fact, it seems more probable that it was a ploy since the next lines state in no uncertain terms that Girish was connected with no theatre other than Classic and that all his new writing would be for Classic. 'Srijukta Girish Chandra now belongs to Classic.' Now Amarendra brought back Tarasundari, Tinkadi, Mahendralal and Danibabu—all the stalwarts of Bengali theatre of the time into Classic.[24]

These glorious days, however, soon passed and internal dissensions and over-expenditure created trouble for Classic. Soon, he was unable to pay many dues including the monthly salary of Girish who immediately left Classic for Minerva.

Classic ushered in many modern stage techniques such as like push scenes, cut scenes, box scenes, changeable wings and proscenium and was the first to introduce the curtain as a drop scene (as claimed by Narendra Deb in the *Ananda Bazar Patrika*, 21st Chaitra, 1347 BS, 1940) while Dharmadas Sur of the Great National Theatre claimed to have introduced the drop scene in his autobiography.[25] Other changes on stage were the use of real furniture in place of packing boxes covered with cloth, the use of wet clothes on actresses and actors to indicate their coming out of rivers, and the use of real water on stage to indicate waterfalls, ponds and fountains. Real animals too were brought on stage such as like horses, dogs and cats. Other innovation included showing sunrises and sunsets, the use of sound and light to portray lightning, the use of wires to show flying through space, use of train noises, the use of real firearms on stage, and the use of real large pleasure boats on stage.

Ostentatious show was the order of the day and in some ways compromises were made with originality. There was the use of high colours instead of real tones, the use of Western-style verandahs, steel engravings on furniture, Western castles instead of Indian forts, villas instead of gardens, corridors, instead of verandahs, drawing room instead of royal courts. Not only was much greater attention paid to dresses, which though it leaned towards extravagance, was an improvement from the lack of variety of the previous age.

All these innovations no doubt brought Amarendranath into the limelight and he could never prevent people from either praising him sky-high nor casting aspersions on his character and work. In fact, those very people whom he entertained at his home, seriously straining his financial resources, always criticized him later. A question that arises in the mind of anyone reading about Amarendranath is: was art or financial success the true motivation behind his gigantic effort? Critics have blamed Amarendranath for his efforts at innovations as having lowered the standard of Bengali theatre and his 'war attempts' against the other theatres as ultimately self-destroying. Kironmoy Raha, in fact, blames the unprofessional and unbusinesslike attitude of Amarendranath for Classic's downfall and maintains that his contribution was much greater in the three theatre journals he created[26] It is true that all his attempts could not prevent the end of Classic in 1906 and nor could he even stop his actors and actresses, not even Girish, from moving to greener pastures. But it is doubtful if such simplistic standards of judgement can be applied to someone who had, so to speak, made so many sacrifices to translate his dream into reality. From a young age, he was willing to forego the peaceful luxurious lifestyle of a scion of a rich and established family for the tough, lonely and uncertain life of a theatre actor or manager. He never wasted any time bemoaning his fate when he was faced with difficulties and he always strove to find a way to overcome it using methods never hitherto tried in the theatrical circles. The very fact that these factors were successful in drawing audiences to his theatres made them seem dubious to conservative Bengali critics. Interestingly, these changes were not that unique, they had already been successfully tried in the Parsi theatres of Bombay and later in Calcutta. It is quite possible that Amarendranath was aware of their techniques. Amarendranath, it is true, used very unconventional tactics which shocked the sensibilities of society, but their instant success forced the other companies to accept that they had to emulate or perish. Whatever 'wrong tactics' Amarendranath was guilty of using were also used by Girish Ghosh, the undisputed teacher of all Bengali actors. This was undoubtedly a vindication of the efficacy of his methods, however dubious they may have been.

The persistent theory that the adoption of management strategies is dangerous and success through this approach has to be at the cost of art needs to be re-examined. Theatre as a performing art needs an audience and for professional theatre, the Box Office is surely an index of success. Where, in fact, I feel that Amarendranath was far more dedicated to art and far less commercial-minded was in his attitude to his own personal survival. What he did not do, unlike many others, was shift loyalties from one theatre to another for personal gain. He fought to preserve a creation of love. Even his personal disappointments like the repeated loss of his mentor Girish Ghosh's support or the betrayal of his lover Tarasundari did not destroy him and neither did it make him swerve from the path of serving his creation or redeeming his promise of improving the conditions of theatre in Bengal and the image and financial condition of the Bengali actor. The only thing he was fighting against was the insistence on 'respectability' but again that was because it was no longer necessary for theatre to retain what Girish had started and what theatre had tried to achieve for so long. Needs had changed and Amarendranath was the instrument through which the winds of change would shape new directions which a new generation would consolidate under Sisir Bhaduri and Ahindra Chowdhury.

Notes

1. Ramapati Dutta, *Rangalaye Amarendranath*, ed. Devjit Bandopadhyay, Kolkata.
2. Aparesh Chandra Mukhopadhyay, *Rangalaye Trish Bachhar*, ed. Swapan Majumdar, Calcutta: Papyrus, 1991.
3. Ramapati Dutta, op. cit., p. 133.
4. Ibid., p. 120.
5. Amarendranath Dutta quoted in Ramapati Dutta, op. cit., p. 138.
6. Aparesh Chandra Mukhopadhayay, *Rangalaye Trish Bochhor*, op. cit., pp. 49–54.
7. Ramapati Dutta, op. cit., p. 139.
8. Quoted in Ramapati Datta, op. cit., p. 138.
9. Ibid., p. 142.
10. Ibid., p. 147.
11. Dev Narayan Gupta, *Banglar Nat Nati*, vol. I, Kolkata: Sahitya Lok, 1985, p. 8.

12. Ajit Kumar Ghosh, *Natyatattva O Natyamancha*, Kolkata: Dey's Publishing, 1991, p. 60.
13. Ajit Kumar Ghosh, op. cit., p. 61.
14. Dwijendralal Roy, Prayaschitta (January 1902), *Dwijendra Racanabali*, vol. I, ed. Rathindra Nath Roy, Calcutta: Sahitya Samsad, 3rd edn., 1985, p. 433.
15. Ajit Kumar Ghosh, *Natyatattva O Natyamancha*, op. cit., p. 69.
16. Ramapati Datta, op. cit., p. 152.
17. Aparesh Chandra Mukhopadhyay, op. cit., pp. 56–7.
18. Advertisement handbill of adaptation of *Kopaal Kundala* by Girish Ghosh in Classic with Amarendranath Dutta as manager, quoted by Ajit Kumar Ghosh, *Natyatatva O Natyamancha*, op. cit., pp. 77–8.
19. Aparesh Chandra Mukhopdhaya op. cit., p. 59.
20. Quoted in Ramapati Datta, op. cit., p. 158.
21. Ibid., p. 219.
22. Quoted in Ramapati Datta, op. cit., p. 171.
23. Ibid., p. 208.
24. Ramapati Datta, op. cit., p. 215.
25. Ajit Kumar Ghosh, *Natyatattva O Natyamancha*, op. cit., p. 122 footnotes.
26. Kironmoy Raha, *Bengali Theatre*, New Delhi: National Book Trust, 1985, p. 63.

6

FIGHT FOR IDENTITY OR SURVIVAL

The Actress at the Law Courts

Defying established practice in nineteenth-century Calcutta, theatre actresses were brought into the public theatre from 1873 in response to the increasing artistic conviction that men were unsuitable for female roles. Since girls from respectable families would not be allowed by their families to perform in public theatre, these actresses had to be brought in from the prostitute families—either prostitutes themselves or living in the same locality. While performances of music and dance by public women before large and even elite audiences was the norm and almost a ritual from time immemorial, yet a social revolution of sorts was created when women entered the theatre. This was because unlike the other forms of entertainment in the theatre, they were performing in close proximity to men from respectable families. Girish Ghosh, the doyen of Bengali theatre said in sadness and disgust, that it 'was only towards theatre that (their) fingers were raised'.[1]

All the debates for or against the inclusion of women in theatre were from the point of view of the men—how middle-class morality was endangered by the proximity or that it was a golden opportunity for society, trying through the light of enlightenment that the colonial cultural encounter had brought, to improve the condition of women—to rehabilitate the 'fallen woman'. There was trepidation in the newspapers regarding the new step that public theatre took in 1873 of introducing actresses in female roles instead of young boys, which had been the practice in the private theatres operating in the houses of the rich and respectable for the past some forty years. Some editorials said that since actresses had not been used for so long, Bengal theatre should step cautiously since society was not yet ready for the new step. Bipin Chandra Pal wrote in his Autobiography that it was in the Brahmo Samaj that the rejection of the use of girls from prostitute families as actresses was very severe.[2] There was even a protest against the presence of some Brahmo ladies in the audience in the contemporary journals. As late as 1900, the defensive note is discernable in the writing of Girish Ghosh. He implores the enlightened men of Bengal to offer constructive suggestions rather than simply criticise or express disgust.[3]

Besides Girish, there were some even among the Brahmo leaders like Sundari Mohon Das who in the words of Bipin Chandra Pal, 'welcomed it as opening an honourable occupation for the class of women from whom our actresses were being drawn'. But the person from the theatre who had created waves was Upendranath Das who, in the hope of rehabilitating famed and successful actress Golaap, better known as Sukumari, married her to an actor of the company called Goshtho Behari Datta. Bipin Chandra Pal, who described the incident of the marriage said in his memoirs, '. . . though the example of these prominent members of the Bengali stage was not followed by others as was expected at the time yet it did to some extent indicate a healthy line of evolution and the very possibility of such unions somewhat removed the moral ban against our stage'.[4] Unfortunately, this optimistic attitude was restricted to some individuals alone and not reflected in society as a whole which led to tragic consequences for the famed marriage.

Thus, there was continuous debate on the actress's effect on society and a consensus was present that they were a necessary evil for improved theatre. But what was never discussed was the new identity that was insidiously developing since that was something which the leaders of society would have been reluctant to admit. For the first time, actresses were vying with men for fame, position and articulation in the newly-created world of theatre. If contemporary literature, journals or even the writings of the actors and actresses of the time are studied, it is evident that there was no acknowledgement of this 'new woman' who stayed in the grey area—not a respectable householder, yet not totally rejected as a prostitute would be, since she was slightly empowered by money and fame. Nowhere was there an articulation or even the admission of an aspiration by the actresses themselves nor by their male patrons or biographers of using the profession as a means to assert their identity as independent women free of the control by the males in their lives. A modern researcher reading between the lines may however identify a faint yet distinct attempt by some of the actresses at least to assert themselves against the 'injustices' perpetrated against them by an patriarchal society which comprised not only the upholders of society's 'virtue' but also the trusted and close—their mentors, teachers, managers, lovers and admirers. It is some of the protests of these actresses that I am going to trace in this paper to see if they were 'uneducated women of easy virtue', asserting their status as artists or simply putting up a fight for survival in a hostile world.

Discussed here are only a few cases of assertion by actresses who were either pitied or vilified by contemporary reports as well as posterity to show that some of them at least were conscious of their rights if not their self-respect. For some of them it was also a fight to stay afloat in the face of stiff competition, while for others going against their mentors or lovers was doubly difficult. Some of these protests reached the courts while others were silenced outside. The most famous actress of the Bengali stage, Binodini Dasi, suffered grave disappointments and betrayal at the hands of her mentor Girish Ghosh, but only resorted to laments in her autobiography.[5] She gave up her loyalty to her lover and literally sold herself to Gurmukh Rai so that Girish could have a new theatre but when Gurmukh promised that the theatre should be in Binodini's name at the last moment, Girish changed the name of B theatre to Star, thereby depriving Binodini. Despite the fact that Binodini commanded not only name and fame but also respect since she had been blessed by the saintly Sri Ramkrishna, she could not take any firm action against Girish Ghosh. Tarasundari, on the other hand, used the courts to fight her battles. It is true that the path to legal use had been taught to her by her mentor/lover, Amarendranath Datta, but later she turned the tables on him. Amarendranath left his home and wife to settle in the family garden-house at Bagmari with Tarasundari, the leading lady of Star. Tara left the home of her mother to live with Amar and possibly on his advice sent a legal notice through Attorney B.N. Mullick to her mother Nityakali Dasi complaining that she had confiscated some of Tara's jewellery and furniture. Nityakali did not reply to the letter till she received a summons from the High Court that Tara had registered a case against her. Nityakali then appeared in court and said that the whole case was false since Tara had run away with all her jewellery and that it was Amarendranath who had enticed her away since she was a minor in the eyes of the law. Tara now realised that she had made a mistake and that she was not going to win the case. She then left Amarendranath and returned to her mother and rejoined Star at a salary of Rs. 32. Amarendranath felt betrayed and in anger sued Tara in the High Court for breach of trust saying that she had taken Rs. 2,000 from him in her legal battle against her mother. He presented a bill of Rs. 2,000 given to attorney Kumud Nath Ganguly at the court. Tara realized that she would have to fight this case out and went to the office of Attorneys Wilson, Mitra and Chatterjee to appear on her behalf. Their defense was that Tara, in the innocence of her youth, had been lured by Amarendranath to his garden-house with the promise of a payment of Rs. 200 a month, which was incredible for an actress at that time. He had also incited her to send a legal notice to her mother and she did not even know what the case had been about.[6] Amarendranath's biographer Ramapati Datta (the alias of his nephew Harindranath) does not even mention this exchange between Tara and Amarendranath and on the contrary concentrates on the interaction between Amar and his family regarding sharing of the property which the family felt he was squandering on Tara while his wife and child suffered.[7] Interestingly, Harindranath, like his father, the elder brother of Amarendranath, though trained in law, ignores this lawsuit though he speaks in details about the later ones. It is obvious he wanted to save the family from social disgrace by discussing his loss of face resulting from the legal action of Tara. The lawsuit must have taken place in the 1890s and Tara rejoined Star on running away from Amarendranath. Later, however, Tara must have forgotten her grievance against Amarendranath since she joined Classic and worked with him. Also from 1904, though she was the mistress of Aparesh Chandra Mukhopadhyay, for the next twenty years, yet Aparesh in his autobiography, *Rangalaye Trish Bachhar*, does not mention the lawsuit, nor seems to have any animosity against Amarendranath.[8]

Another case study where an actress came into direct confrontation with a theatre was Sushilabala, who from 1893 was associated with Minerva though not continuously and was such an asset to the theatre due to her talent as a singer that she was called *Prima Donna Nightingale*. It was this talent that got her into trouble. While working for Minerva in a number of plays by Dwijendralal Roy where her singing prowess made her a darling of the audience, she got an offer from National

Theatre in 1906 for a bonus of Rs. 1,000 and an increased salary of Rs. 120, Rs. 20 more than what she was being paid by Minerva. Whether she knew that this was a flagrant defiance of her legal contract with Minerva is not known but what is known is that she was in dire straits since Narendranath, the zamindar of Sripur with whom she lived like a married couple from around the beginning of the twetienth century, filed for insolvency in 1901 and Sushilabala, who had given up the theatre for two years, had to rejoin to earn a living.[9] Anyhow, when Monomohon Pandey of Minerva got to know about her contract with the National Theatre they asked her to tear up the contract and offered her a bonus of Rs. 1,000 and an increase of Rs. 10 to her salary. This new contract was for three years. Unfortunately, according to Debnarayan Gupta, they did not let her act in the majority of their plays, probably as punishment, though she had shown her mettle as a singing star previously. In the meantime, Dwijendralal who had a fight with Star, offered his play *Rana Pratap* to Minerva and it was advertised that Sushilabala was to play the lead part of Meherunnisa. At this time, the manager, Monomohan Pandey, got a letter from Sushilabala recounting this entire episode and stating that she had signed a stamped paper contract without being fully aware of what was written and that she felt that the contract was not in her favour and so wished to be freed of her obligations in Minerva. This was a double blow for Minerva since it was two days before the opening night and they believed that the letter had been engineered by the management of Star. The play was postponed and all the tickets were refunded, while a lawsuit was filed against Sushilabala in the High Court demanding a compensation of Rs. 10,000. Monomohon Pandey submitted Sushilabala's original contract with Minerva where she had promised to stay for three years on a salary of Rs. 100 and stating that she could not join any other theatre openly or in secret. The third clause was that since she was accepting a bonus of Rs. 1,000 she could not leave Minerva at any cost. This contract had her signature, Srimati Sushilabala Dasi dated 1313 BS, 24 paus. In the hearing, Monomohon Pandey said Sushilabala had learnt all that she knew about acting from Girish Ghosh at Minerva and that Minerva had suffered severe losses since they could not finally stage *Rana Pratap* due to her defection, and that she must compensate for the loss. Minerva had also signed with one Guruprasad Singh for performances for many nights which too had to be cancelled. Monomohon also alleged that Sushilabala had betrayed Minerva and joined the new Kohinoor Theatre. Sushilabala appeared in court and negated the rumour that she had joined another theatre. She had asked Minerva to let her off quite privately and it was to get her into trouble that she had suddenly, after being ignored for so long, been given a leading part. She also alleged that a trustee Mahendra Kumar Mitra had made an immoral proposition to her which had offended her so much that she had decided to quit. Ramen Gupta, who has discussed this case, takes an unsympathetic view of the actress as simply trying to get out of an illegal act by making an allegation against a man with whom she had been having an affair anyway.[10] However, another biographer on the actress takes a more sympathetic view saying that though successful as an actress, Sushilabala still retained the stigma of a prostitute and this went against her in court.[11] In any event, none of her pleas worked and on 17 February 1908, the Judge Fletcher passed a verdict saying that till her contract ended, Sushilabala would continue to work for Mineva and would have to pay the expenditure incurred by Minerva during the legal battle. Sushilabala appealed against the verdict, but it was to no avail and Judges Maclean and Harrington dismissed the appeal. Sushilabala was forced to swallow her pride and stay on for some more time. But she was so successful in her performances that in 1911, Amarendranath Dutta, who opened the Great National Theatre, offered her a bonus of Rs. 3,000 and an alternative haven. Sushilabala's strength of character acting was legendary and it has often been pointed out that Dwijendralal preferred casting her in his plays because they had female roles requiring both acting and singing talent.[12]

Two court cases involving actresses in the late 1920s, Kankabati Sahoo and Charushila, also involved the legendary actor Sisir Bhaduri. The nature of his involvement in the two cases were exactly opposite but both caused great excitement in the contemporary journals and newspapers since they involved such a well-known and erudite theatre personality. In 1928, many posters were displayed on the streets of Calcutta mentioning that the Star Theatre had acquired the services of Kankabati Sahoo, incidentally the first graduate actress of public theatre and coming from a respectable background with a Zamindar and an honorary Magistrate for a father who took on the responsibility of bringing her up when her actress mother died. One can imagine the excitement that had been created with the advertisement posters on Kankaboti—a respectable and educated woman joining a den of vice with her father's permission was unheard of.[13] Around this time, the manager Probodh Guha received a letter from the actress Kankaboti that though she had no contract with Art Theatre, yet her name was displayed in the posters. Probodh Guha sued her in the High Court to the effect that she had signed a three-year contract to act in Star and that together with actor-director Sisir Bhaduri of Natya Mandir, she had concocted this story that there was no contract. Probodh Guha demanded both Sisir Bhaduri and Kaonkaboti should pay him Rs. 10,000 each. At the hearing at the High Court in his statement, the secretary of Star Theatre, Biswanath Chakraborty, said that he was a witness to Kankaboti's signing of the contract and that after a few rehearsals she feigned illness and on the pretext of resting went to Natyamandir where she rehearsed in plays with Sisir Bhaduri. Another witness on Probodh Guha's side, Bimalapada Pal, a jute businessman who knew Kankaboti and her actress mother said that he had heard about this dangerous game that she was playing with Star and Natyamandir and warned her about it and alleged that Kankaboti claimed that she had signed a contract with Sisir Bhaduri. Aparesh Mukhopadhyay, writer and actor, associated with the Star also said that he has been present when Kankaboti signed the contract with Star. After that, Sisir Bhaduri entered centre-stage in court where he tore Probodh Guha's image into shreds. Before joining Star, he had been a clerk at the Post and Telegraph department from where he had been dismissed. Also, Sisir Bhaduri alleged that before the liquidation of the Bengal National Bank, Probodh had taken overdrafts not only in his name but also in the name of the other actresses of Star as well as his mistress Niharbala. Sisir Bhaduri also said that a proposal had been made to him to merge Star and Natyamandir but that he had insisted that he was willing for the merger if a guarantee could be given to him that the notorious Probodh Guha would not be associated with the theatre. The present case had been set up, he alleged, out of that anger. He also proved with witnesses that Kankaboti had approached him to only learn the art of acting and had not been allotted any part in any play and there was no contract. Kankaboti in her statement spoke about her background, how her mother Nalinibala who had been an actress with Star, had come into contact with the Zamindar Gadadhar Sahoo of Bihar and had borne him several children. After her mother's death, their father had always been supportive though he had not been able to give them social recognition. Her moving statement created great excitement in court and tilted the judgement in her favour. Star was asked to retract any contract that had been signed with Kankabati but she had to wait for the rest of the year before joining any theatre group, though she could act in films. After that, if she joined any professional theatre, she could not advertise her entry.[14] Despite these restrictions, the case went resoundingly in her favour. Later, she came closer to Sisir Bhaduri and became his life-partner.

Charushila's case was, on the contrary, a stigma for Sisir Bhaduri but a triumph for the actress. The *Advance* newspaper published in two episodes a small drama enacted in the courtroom when Charushila of his dramatic company sued Sisir Kumar for unpaid dues. On 26 August 1930, a report on *Theatrical artist in trouble—Bhaduri not to go to America?* said that 'at the Calcutta high Court, before Mr Justice Costello, Mr Sudhir Roy, made an application on behalf of the plaintiff Srimati Charusila Dassi, an actress, for issue of a writ of arrest against the defendant, Sisir Kumar Bhaduri, a well known actor and for an injunction restraining him from leaving the jurisdiction of the court. It was alleged that Rs. 2188-9-0 was due to her from the defendant for arrears of salary which the defendant failed to pay. She also claimed Rs. 157-8-0 as damages for wrongful dismissal.' The case not being resolved, the court ordered the defendant, Sisir Kumar, not to leave the city before the next hearing which was scheduled to be held the week after. This was specified because it was established in court that he was about to leave for America in mid-September to stage several Bengali plays.[15] On 29 August, a report was made that Judge Panckridge 'had disposed of the rule issued on behalf of Charusila Dassi calling upon Sj. S.K.Bhaduri to show cause why an injunction should not be issued restraining him from proceeding to America'. S.C. Roy on behalf of the applicant said that she had not prayed for a warrant but wanted that the defendant furnish security before leaving India so that the execution of the decree might not be delayed. Mr S.M. Bose for Sj. Bhaduri submitted that 'there were no circumstances showing that his object was to delay the execution of the decree. He was leaving for America as he had got an offer.... He was going there with his party and was expected to come back after 2 or 3 months. Counsel submitted there was something behind the application.' The ulterior motive was indicated as being jealousy because though some actresses were chosen to go to America with Bhaduri, Charu was not one of them. 'His Lordship directed the defendant Bhaduri to furnish security of Rs. 2,000 to the applicant to the satisfaction of the Registrar. If he failed to furnish the security, warrant might be issued against him and the interim injunction would continue till the security was furnished.'[16] *Advance* does not clarify whether Sisir Kumar actually paid the security but the fact that he sailed for America on 8 September makes one presume that he paid Charushila the security. Thus, Sisir Bhaduri, who in Kankaboti's case was able to turn the case around, was not quite successful in this case. However, he did try to outwit Charushila when he filed a case against her and the trustee of Minerva, Upendranath Mitra, in the High Court for breach of contract. He claimed that she had joined Minerva while still bound by contract to Natyamandir. He therefore demanded Rs. 15,000 from them as compensation and asked that the court declare an injunction on Charushila so that she would not be able to perform in Minerva till her contract period was over. Charushila in retaliation presented a list of the creditors to whom Sisir Bhaduri owed money and claimed that once Natyamandir closed down, she was not bound by any contract. She also alleged that it was to escape his financial burden that Sisir Bhaduri was escaping to America.[17]

What is noticeable is that the strength of character in an actress is not proportionate to her fame or position in the theatre world. Binodini Dasi, though the most famous actress of her time, could not take a stern step against her mentor other than make insinuations in her autobiography, Tarasundari, another legendary figure, second only to Binodini, acquitted herself very well in the court against Amarendranath, using very plausible arguments about her extreme youth and gullibility against a rich, charming and talented mentor. Her victory was definitely a devastating blow to society because Amarendranath had smeared the proverbial ink on the face of his family prestige to live a lavish life with Tara. So it is not surprising that the episode was swept under the carpet by all the men concerned and that even contemporary journals do not mention it. But it is indeed strange how Tara herself played a part in this when she seemed to forget her sufferings and the humiliation of having to retract her words and action against her mother before the court when she rejoined Amarendranath in his new ventures. It is even more surprising that her partner Aparesh Mukhopadhyay, writer and actor, does not mention the duel between Tara and Amarendranath and in fact is repeatedly very appreciative of the new tactics that Amarendranath applied to theatre in order to increase Box Office sales against other established theatres. It is as if the court case from which

Amarendranath withdrew in shame and defeat just did not happen. If, as is generally alleged, actresses always chose monetary benefit over truth, then Tara must have been extremely stupid if she chose her mother's support and company over that of the rich patron who later started his own theatre company and became the manager of two theatres simultaneously as well as editing a theatre journal. It is true that he later suffered financial losses but Tara was not to know this till much later. In fact, at that time, Amarendranath had offered her far more than Star, and yet she chose to abandon her lover. This is as intriguing as her later return to Classic, having wiped the slate clean.

Unlike in the case of Tara who was confronting a famous actor and director plus the son of a well-known and established family with a lawyer for a brother, and it being obvious that all efforts would be made by the family to keep his reputation intact, and with the contemporary journals in the last decade of the nineteenth century probably siding with him rather than with an actress of shifting loyalties, the next cases aroused sympathy in contemporary writing. Sushilabala's case has been discussed by her biographers in sympathy that such a great actress had to face the ignominy of defeat in a legal battle with a theatre manager. This could be since in the eyes of society and theatre-lovers, the position of the manager who was not an actor was even below that of the actress. What is generally overlooked is that Sushilabala was fighting alone against male domination in the theatre and was fighting for survival since her patron/partner was insolvent and unable to provide for them. Though Sushilabala had, as was the practice at that time, given up working in the theatre when she started living with the Zamindar of Sripur, she rejoined her profession as the bread-winner. She was, in fact, loved not only as a talented actress and singer, but also respected for her strong personality. That is why it was pointed out by one of her biographers Debnarayan Gupta that it was her personality that inspired Dwijendralal Roy to base a portrayal of one of his characters on her (Shanta in *Parapare*).[18]

While histrionics did not work for Sushilabala, who was fighting without the backing of a strong male, Kankaboti Shahoo had all the qualities that created romance. She was the highly-educated, daughter of a rich Zamindar, the daughter of an established actress and protégée of an acclaimed actor, director, educator Sisir Bhaduri, who later married her. Not only did he intelligently prove that the accuser himself was a corrupt man, thereby exposing him to the disdain of the jury, but

Kankaboti's tearful portrayal of her difficult life after her mother's death and how, despite her father's love and encouragement she could not get social recognition, was convincing. Professional fame was the only way for her to achieve a position in society and to make her father proud. Besides, she had only been fighting against the injustice of domination by an established theatre. Also, she had not yet joined Natyamandir or Kohinoor as alleged.

Charushila's case was discussed prominently in the contemporary newspapers since Sisir Bhaduri's invitation to America and his subsequent successes and failures were avidly followed by his audience in India. So, a court case at an opportune moment which could have jeopardized his sojourn was bound to make news. What one cannot understand from the reporting in *Advance* is whether social backing was for the great Sisir Bhaduri on his way to conquer America or for Charushila who was in dire straits, not having been given her dues and also having been left out of the forthcoming voyage. One presumes that Mr Bhaduri paid off his outstanding dues since the next reporting is on his success at the performance in New York and how he had been duped by his sponsors.

It is true that in this period there were a number of court cases by women, sometimes with the backing of a man and sometimes by themselves, generally regarding fraud in cash or property. Some examples are Gauhar Jaan against her lover, husband and manager Abbas Ali where she had to prove her parentage or lose all her property,[19] or in the case of Lakshimoni, the prostitute's daughter, who did not want to follow her mother's profession and was involved in a case where her mother charged a Brahmo reformer Nabakanta Chattopadhyay with kidnapping.[20] In the case of the actress it was often against a stronger opponent who mostly had the backing of a theatre and the support of the leading men of the society.

Notes

1. *Girish Rachnabali*, vol. I, ed. Rathindra Nath Roy and Devipada Bhattacharya, Calcutta: Sahitya Samsad, 1991, 3rd edn., pp. 735–6, first published in Rangalaya, 17th Falgun, 1307 BS.
2. Bipin Chandra Pal, *Memories of My Life and Times*, Calcutta: Bipin Chandra Pal Institute, 2nd revised edn., 1973, pp. 242–3.
3. *Girish Racanabali*, vol. I, p. 736.
4. Bipin Chandra Pal, *Memories of My Life and Times*, op. cit., pp. 242–3.

5. Binodini Dasi, *Amar Kotha O Onanyo Rochona*, ed. Soumitra Chattopadhyay and Nirmalya Acharya, Calcutta: Subarnarekha, repr. 1987.
6. Ramen Gupta, *Green Room Theke Court Room*, Calcutta: Papyrus, 1992, pp. 36–7.
7. Ramapati Datta, *Rangalaye Amarendranath*, originally published in 1940, and republished by Debjit Bandopadhyay, Calcutta: Dey's Publishing, 2004. In his editorial comments and footnotes, he mentions the case and the *Rangalaye Nati*, peculiar silence of Ramapati Datta.
8. Aparesh Chandra Mulhopadhyay, *Rangalaye Trish Bachhar*, Calcutta, 1935, Publisher unknown.
9. Debnarayan Gupta, *Banglar Natnati*, vol. I, Kolkata: Sahityalok, 1985, pp. 98–9.
10. Ramen Gupta, *Green Room Theke Court Room*, op. cit., p. 51.
11. Amit Maitra, *Rangalaye Nati*, Kolkata: Ananda, 2004, p. 289.
12. Debnarayan Gupta, *Banglar Natnati*, vol. I, op. cit., pp. 101–2.
13. Amit Maitra, *Rangalaye Nati*, op. cit., p. 686.
14. Ramen Gupta, *Green Room Theke Court Room*, op. cit., pp. 89–94.
15. *Advance*, Tuesday, 26 August 1930.
16. Ibid., Friday, 29 August 1930.
17. Ramen Gupta, *Green Room Theke Court Room*, op. cit., pp. 103–9.
18. Debnarayan Gupta, *Banglar Natnati*, vol. I, op. cit., pp. 98–9.
19. Vikram Sampat, *My Name is Gauhar Jaan': Life and Times of a Musician*, New Delhi: Rupa & Co., 2010, pp. 171–82.
20. Sumanta Banerjee, Asruta Kanthaswar, Kolkata: Subarnarekha, 2002, pp. 62–9.

7

SEARCH FOR A NEW SPACE

Artistic Identity or a New 'Family'

THE GREATEST DILEMMA that an actress confronted when she joined the theatre was whether she was looking for survival in monetary terms or whether artistic perfection was a means in itself. The fact that she came not from within the safe refuge of a normal family but from the harsh environment of the prostitute quarters made it difficult to ignore the need for stability. The women knew from the harsh realities of their environment that their fame or success in the theatrical world was transient and so they would have to prepare for their future. In a sense, they were far worse off than their compatriots in the forbidden quarters of the city since the latter did not have to fight off a stigma nor try to train in their accent, behaviour, or attitude not to speak of acting, singing and dancing styles. These actresses had to forget their backgrounds and learn to act as characters they never knew existed. But their limited education and poverty-stricken homes never acted as a barrier in their vibrant desire to learn. They learned to take pride in themselves and their work but at the same time became dependent on their tutor-patrons.

Girish said in his *Banga-Rangalaye Srimati Binodini* that he had asked Binodini to write her memoirs so that it might be an inspiration to improve herself through remembering the process as well as be an inspiration to other women like her. But he was reluctant to write a preface to her account when she requested him to since he was not sure how one should defend oneself to the reader. He said he did not like the fact that Binodini bemoaned her fate and presented her memoirs as her life's tragedy. He had probably wanted her book to be an inspirational example for others to follow. He was probably embarrassed at the many instances that Binodini showed of betrayal by her theatrical connections and even him. He tried to sidetrack by pointing out that her sadness was because of her background which kept haunting her till the end and even prevented her daughter from being educated like children from other respectable families. Ultimately, he changed his mind about writing the preface when, as he said, he realised that if other women could read how Binodini had received the blessings of the greatest living saint in India of the time despite coming from such a fallen family, they might be inspired to join the theatre. What many devotees could not achieve despite years of devotion, Binodini was able to through her performance. If her life could be an example to society, then she would not have lived in vain.

Girish Ghosh thereby equated acting in a theatre to the piety of a householder for whom daily prayers were a part of life. This not only removed the stigma from a profession vilified by contemporary writers but also in the same stroke empowered it through a connection with divinity. If the sage Ramkrishna could perceive the divine in the acting of Binodini, there must be something right in bringing in these women to deliver themselves from their degraded existence through art. 'Those who like Binodini were unfortunate enough to belong to a family which had no other alternative livelihood, those who are being wooed by sweet nothings by men of loose morals, even they will be inspired. . . . Those who are actresses will realize that if they concentrate on a superlative performance in the roles allotted to them they will be feted by the society—it was this thought that compelled me to write the preface to Binodini's book.'[1] Yet he remained ignorant of the fact that Binodini was able to stay an inspiration for generations of actresses to come because her account of her life made her effort believable, the weaknesses and bemoaning of fate that he condemned made her beloved of all those women who faced innumerable instances of humiliation and discrimination. What came across for posterity was not helplessness but an acceptance of her limitations and a sense of self respect and pride in her achievements. She faced repeated betrayals from those whom she loved and admired but she dealt with her pain with a wry sense of humour. As she wrote in *Amar Abhinetri Jiban* (*My Life as an Actress*), she received 'at least two or three offers of fifty thousand rupees' (in return for the favours of a mistress or a wife) but she 'spurned them like dust' so enchanted was she by the magic of theatre.[2]

Girish has criticised in his preface the writing style of Binodini when he writes that 'she has not discussed the events in her life properly but is only looking for sympathy'. At times she has strongly criticised society which has embarrassed him. He also felt that she has 'spoken only about herself' and has not given details of how she trained for each role, 'how each effort paid dividends, how important discipline was, how (her) voice was trained, how attention was paid to every action'. What I feel rather is that the memoirs were, as Girish must have realised even then, a skilful protest against all the injustices committed by Girish and others towards Binodini.

The Opposing Stream—The Mind of the Actress

It is true that training by the great personalities of the time were for both actors and actresses. Yet in the case of the actress there seems to be a difference. A kind of mystical aura surrounded the teacher-pupil relationship in the Guru-shishya style which became a bond for life. This extended beyond the stage to guidance in day-to-day life. This could be because the actors came from secure middle class backgrounds though once they entered the 'tainted' portals of the theatre they were more or less forced to sever connections with their families. The actresses on the other hand were stepping into the unknown once they left the shelter of their erstwhile profession. They not only had to portray unfamiliar roles on stage in front of a critical audience but also had to carry on living public lives off-stage especially once they became famous. So in this unfamiliar terrain the bona fide protection that a cult figure offered must have been irresistible.

The actresses are very voluble in the expression of their gratitude to their teachers, and mentors. Throughout her writings, Binodini's gratitude towards Girish Ghosh, her mentor, is evident. Sushilabala, another actress, protested strongly when the actresses were not granted permission to publicly express their respect at the memorial service of Girish Ghosh in Town Hall. Under her leadership, the leading actresses of the day organised another such service at the Star Theatre on 18 September 1912, presided over by Amarendranath. Why should it be that because they were 'fallen women' their expression of respect for their teacher is considered a 'mere show'? Girish babu was according to her a Guru, father and teacher who spread the light of knowledge into their hearts, and taught them to earn money through hard labour.[3] Other actresses who expressed their gratitude to Girish were Rani Sundari and Narisundari who said that they owed their success to Girish Ghosh. Narisundari praised her mentor Girish as having not only trained her in becoming an actress, understanding the various nuances of every role and performing them in the best possible way, not only for having written plays which would give much happiness and moral teachings, but also because of having given her an alternative life than the one she was born to. As she put it, society had forsaken her at birth for being born with a stigma but unlike the 'saints' who did not hesitate to slander and hate her, Girish who was much nobler than those 'saints' was able to rise above the established views and help her to enact Nitai in *Chaitanyaleela* and Pagolini in *Bilwamangal*. She recalls with gratitude that, thanks to Girish, she was able to recite the praises of Sri Chaitanyadev and lower her head at the feet of Sri Ramkrishna who visited the theatre to watch the play.[4]

The result of this dependence was a blurring of the lines demarcating personal lives and careers. It would have been understandable if it had been only their teacher and theatre mentor who was taking decisions for these women since they had almost given them new lives, but often we notice that even successful actresses often let those men who provided them security and were not associated with the theatre take important decisions for them, even depriving them of their acting career which brought them fame and monetary escape from the drudgery of their past lives. In their urgency to flee the 'shame' of their past life, they often floundered in their career choices, depending on the whims and limitations of their patrons. Their career graph often fluctuated with the personal fortunes of these men. If the supporters of the use of actresses in Bengali theatre believed that the acting profession would be the saviour of all these degraded women by granting them respectability, they had miscalculated. They did not take into account the emotional factors. These women always placed love and loyalty for individuals above their careers. Some considered domesticity a better alternative than a career on stage while for others, even in their career choices, priority was always given to the patrons' wishes.

As illustration I will take up some case studies to show how important decisions of the actresses were influenced by others. I start with the greatest actress of the Bengali stage, Binodini Dasi. Binodini's attachment to her mentor Girish Ghosh was legendary. She called herself his right hand and said that he rushed to fulfil all her trivial whims. She attributed her success in theatre to Girish Ghosh. But his influence did not end there. In most of her personal decisions he played a role, sometimes supporting her wishes and at other times impressing upon her that his decision would benefit her. Quite early in her career, the young man who looked after her wanted her to leave the theatre. Then, realising that Binodini was too committed to acting to heed his request, he asked her not to accept a salary for her performance. This too went against her independent spirit. Finally, on the advice of Girish Ghosh, she pretended to be an honorary artist and her salary was given to her mother. Another occasion when Binodini had to go against her conscience was when on the advice of her Guru she had to accept the offer of Gurmukh Rai as her patron though she still felt attached to her previous patron. At this juncture, when Gurmukh offered her Rs. 50,000 in lieu of the theatre, she resisted the temptation. That would have meant leaving the profession she adored. But to save her mentor, Girish, and other actors who had been left without a theatre to perform in, she had to compromise and leave her lover to whom she had been very attached, and accept Gurmukh's offer to be his mistress in lieu of the new theatre that he would build. While making this sacrifice she consoled herself that having a theatre named after her would compensate for her grief. But her hopes were dashed when during the registration, the theatre was named Star and not B theatre, at Girish's instigation. Later, when shares of Star were being bought up, Gurmukh Rai offered to give Binodini some shares, but Girish Ghosh advised her against it saying that a woman would not be able to handle the responsibility.[5]

Tinkadi Dasi is an interesting example of a woman who came into theatre for the love the art and allowed nothing to stand in the way. She was not brought to the theatre by anybody. From her childhood, she had a fascination for the theatre and after repeated requests forced her mother to take her to see a play when she was only seven. Soon afterwards, she convinced Rajkrishna Roy of the Beena Theatre to give her a role. She was convinced that theatre was her life. She rejected her mother's pleas to give up acting and become the mistress of a rich man. The two gentlemen who wanted to become her patrons were promising to pay her a maintenance of the same amount she received as from the theatre every month plus an additional compensation for her mother. But Tinkadi refused to take the easy way out. She preferred the uncertainties of the theatre to the promise of security by the 'Babu'. Neither cajoling nor punishment from her mother swayed Tinkadi's decision to continue with acting. Yet, she had so much self-respect that when she felt insulted by the authorities of the Emerald Theatre in which she worked after Beena, she left without a tremor. This insult was a suggestion by the authorities that her salary be slightly reduced to Rs. 25 from Rs. 40. Despite the threat that she might not get a better offer from any other theatre, Tinkadi resigned. She was overwhelmed when, some years later, she was successfully performing at the City Theatre, Girish Ghosh himself sent an offer to Tinkadi to work under his direction at Minerva. In fact, Girish had given her a smaller salary of Rs. 30 compared to the one she was getting when she quit Emerald. Yet Tinkadi had no hesitation in accepting the contract Girish made her sign with Minerva. He was an inspiration to anyone who wanted to make theatre their life. Tinkadi knew that money would never compensate for what she would learn from Girish's closeness.

Despite their dependence on the theatre mentors, the actresses often showed aggression when they felt thwarted, as in the cases of Charushila and Tarasundari who resorted to court cases when they felt that they were being cheated. Charushila sued Sisir Bhaduri, who despite non-payment of salary due to her, was taking his troupe to New York conveniently leaving Charushila behind. It is not true that these actresses always had sincere motives and were always without malice, but the point is that their public status empowered them much more than their 'respectable' sisters and provided them publicity during their trials, gave them an opportunity to demonstrate a strong position often without open male guardian support. Of course, in most cases, they had strong advisors in the form of men and women who provided them with financial and mental support.

IMPORTANCE OF 'FAMILY TIES' FOR THE ACTRESSES

The social reformers wanted to remove the actresses from their families and put them in a new surrounding where fame and financial security would compensate for the loss or lack of family bindings. It is doubtful if their project succeeded with even a single actress. All the evidence one can glean from contemporary sources speaks loudly of the longing of the actress for love commitments and family ties. Most of them also did not cut off their family connections and fell back on them in times of need. Binodini constantly mentions her mother and grandmother with gratitude and Girish Ghosh actually had to repeatedly win over her mother to his side whenever Binodini asserted her personality and wishes. Also noteworthy was Binodini's loyalty to her patrons and her expectations in return. Binodini was being wooed by Gurmukh Rai who promised the actors of the National Theatre a new theatre only if Binodini became his. But Binodini was tied to another. Then that 'rich youth' played Binodini false by marrying to please his family without informing her. Binodini was furious. 'I began to think that he who had given me the protection had been bound to me by truth. Yet he had broken his word and deceived me . . . He had sworn repeatedly, by all that is dharma, that I was the sole object of his love and his love or me was eternal.' 'I had been deeply affected by this incident. I felt, therefore, that since God had given me the means to earn my living and if I am capable of taking care of myself and the expenses of my family through my physical exertions, I need not add to my burden of sins by selling my body and torment myself besides. If a playhouse could be put together through my offices, then it would forever afford me a source of sustenance.'[6] But, of course, she had to accept Gurmukh Rai as her patron as per the contract till he was forced by his family to sell off his shares of Star and give up Binodini. Finally, when Binodini left the theatre, she combined her two families, staying with her unnamed patron and daughter and bringing her mother to stay with them. She makes a tearful dedication of her book to her late patron.

Tinkadi, who was such a professional actress, became totally unreasonable on one occasion. She was supposed to appear on stage as a widow in *Karameti*, and realised that the 'Babu' she was living with was in the hall. She forgot that she was an actress and refused to appear before him in widow's dress in case it cast a shadow on his life. The theatre authorities averted any mishap by quietly requesting that man to leave the auditorium. Tinkadi later apologized to Girish for her momentary lapse. Gradually, she became Girish's loyal protegee moving from theatre to theatre with him. There were rumours of them living together. In Tinkadi's later life, in sharp contrast to her early years, there were at least two occasions when she was willing to leave acting and it was Girish Ghosh who advised her not to quit. There was a clash between her love and loyalty for her teacher and a rich man who wanted to be her patron. This man of north Calcutta wanted to give shelter to Tinkadi, but on condition that she left theatre. On Girish Ghosh's advice, she rejected the offer. Later, this aggrieved man made an attempt on the lives of Girish Ghosh and Tinkadi, but the attempt was foiled. Somehow, their friend Rajen Chattopadhyay recognised the thug who had been sent to kill Girish and kidnap Tinkadi during an entertainment programme. They were smuggled out and the rich man's plot foiled. There were many such stories illustrative of the close relationship between Girish and Tinkadi and Girish was openly appreciative of her talent. Later, when she fell ill and her diabetic condition forced her to stay away from theatre, Girish advised her to stay in touch with acting by performing occasionally at the Thespian Theatre.[7] The interesting part is that despite the close relationship with Girish, Tinkadi always remained loyal to her 'babu' and according to her will, two of her houses were donated to Mayo Hospital and one to the son of her 'babu'.

Sushilabala, called Prima Donna, or Rangamancher Bulbul also followed the ups-and-downs in the career of her patron Narendranath Sarkar, the Zamindar of Sripur. The first occasion of the display of her loyalty occurred when, after a disagreement between her teacher Girish Ghosh and her patron, she left Minerva in 1900 soon after her first success. She was such a noted singer that she would have got a job in any theatre, but as Narendranath had been declared insolvent and could not get a job anywhere, she also did not accept any. Many offers came to Sushilabala since she was at the height of her career but she did not want to join without Narendranath. They stayed away from theatre as long as they could but then penury drove her to perform again. After many reverses in Minerva, she was able to shake off her contract and join the Great National and Star Theatre in 1911, when the authorities gave Narendranath a job as Editor. Despite all the compromises she made, she excelled in her performances and singing and sometimes had to sing a particular song seven or eight times on public demand. She stayed loyal to Narendranath through all his bad times till the end and bore him a child who died at birth. She was also well-known and admired for her strength of character and Dwijendralal is said to have based the role of Shanta in *Parapare* on Sushilabala.[8]

The unobstrusive role of Tarasundari's mother in her volte face case against Amarendranath needs to be noted. Intitally, the case that Tara had made was possibly on the instigation and definitely with the money of Amarendranath, but then she suddenly changed her mind when she remembered her mother's strained situation and in a total turnaround left Amarendranath and joined her mother. This is so similar to the case of Lakshmoni, a prostitute's daughter in Dhaka, who educated herself and did not want to continue in her mother's profession. She managed to get the help of a local Brahmo social worker, Nabakanto Chattopadhyay and despite a case filed by her mother, was exonerated by an English Judge. She was brought to Calcutta and admitted to a girls' Normal School. However, the stigma of her birth followed her to the city and in her loneliness and rejection it was her mother that she kept missing. In 1874–5 she finally returned to her mother. However, despite her sympathy for her mother's situation Lakshmimoni was 'saved' by the intervention of Sibnath Sastri who married her in 1876 through Brahmo rites to Vishnucharan Chattopadhyay.[9] The mother–daughter tic as evident from both the cases, despite all odds, remained strong and leads to inexplicable actions on the part of the daughters who managed to escape the seediness of their past life, yet retain their sympathy for their mother who despite overwhelming adversity, had brought them up.

Finally, we look at the tragedy of Golaap/Sukumari's marriage. She was one of the first four to join the stage in 1873. It was her talent as a singer that first attracted the notice of Sarat Chandra Ghosh who brought her to the Bengal Theatre. Under the training of Ardhendu Sekhar, she excelled and her talent bloomed. In Upendranath Das' *Sarat Sarojini*, Golaap's performance as Sukumari was so brilliant that she became identified with that character and came to be known henceforth as Sukumari. Upendranath Das in his mission to rehabilitate the actresses, married her to an actor of the group, Goshtho Behari Dutta. Knowing that society would not forgive him for his folly in marrying a fallen woman, Golaap quit her association with theatre. She started living in a shanty with her husband and a daughter was soon born to them. Her troubles, however, did not end since her husband was ostracized by his conservative family. But her sacrifice in giving up her career when it was at its height was in vain as her marriage did not last. With the departure of their ailing mentor Upendranath for London, Goshtho Behari felt unable to withstand societal pressure and, leaving his wife and small daughter behind, he too ran away. In severe financial distress, Golaap turned to her last resort, the theatre. She first made an abortive attempt to start a theatrical group. Then she wrote a play, *Apurba Sati* which according to Atul Krishna Mitra,[10] she co-authored with her manager Ashubabu. Finally, she returned to acting in the Bengal, National, Great National and Emerald Theatres, the grand public reform attempt having proved to be a mirage.

Bengali Theatre in the late nineteenth–twentieth century witnessed the dichotomy between personal security and career satisfaction in the actress. Unlike in England, where the actress, despite becoming the mistress of the leading men of the court or even the royal family, continued to shine in her profession, in Bengal, shelter by a rich patron invariably included a demand to quit the theatre. There are instances in England of married actors and actresses or even siblings performing on stage, but that was unthinkable here. The stigma attached to acting was so severe and the longing for respectability and social acceptance so ingrained in the middle-class mentality of that age that the two were incompatible. However, much Girish might want to rehabilitate the prostitutes as great actresses, he too always talked of redeeming their 'sinful souls' through the blessings of Sri Ramkrishnadev. But he was a champion and a spokesperson for the performer. He deplored the attitude of society which uses the skill of the performer for their own varied purposes but never gives them their due. He speaks of an old man who all his life derided the morality of the actresses of the stage, but who on his death-bed asked his son to call a stage actress to sing devotional songs.[11] The 'private' longings of the public women remained unheard by a rigid society and only rarely expressed in words. Binodini seems to echo the heart of every actress when she says, 'Do we not desire a husband's love? But where are we to find it? Who will give their hearts in return for our own? There is no lack of those who come greedily to talk to us of love, hoping all the while to seduce us, but is there one who would put his heart to the test and find out whether we have anything like a heart? Has anyone ever sought to know whether it was we who first deceived or whether we learnt deception only after we were ourselves deceived?'[12]

Notes

1. *Girish Racanabali*, vol. V, ed. Debipada Bhattacharya, Calcutta: Sahitya Samsad, 2nd edn., 1991 pp. 364–5.
2. Binodini Dasi, Amar Abhinetri Jiban, originally serialized in *Rup O Ranga* (1924–5) repr. *Shatabdir Natyachinta*, ed. Debashish Majumdar and Sekhar Samaddar, Kolkata: A. Mukherjee and Company Pvt Ltd., 2000, p. 38.
3. Harindranath Dutta, 'The Divine Sushila', *Abhinay*, November 1978–9.

4. Star Theatre Smriti Sabha, *Natyamandir*, 3rd year, 2–4 samkhya, Aswin–Kartik, 1319 BS.
5. Binodini Dasi, *Amar Katha O Ananya Racana*, ed. Saumitra Chattopadhyay and Nirmalya Acharya, Calcutta: Subarnarekha, 1987, repr., pp. 37, 40, 46.
6. Binodini Dasi, *My Story and My Life as an Actress*, op. cit., pp. 84–5.
7. Devnarayan Gupta, *Banglar Natnati*, Calcutta: Sahitya Lok, 1985, pp. 61–73.
8. Devnarayan Gupta, ibid., p. 102.
9. Sumanta Bandopadhyay, *Asruta Kanthaswar*, Calcutta: Subarnarekha, 2002, pp. 62–6.
10. Atul Krishna Mitra, Prabina O Nabina, *Rangamancha*, Bhadra, 1317 BS.
11. Girish Ghosh, *Nater Abedan, Girish Racanabali,* vol.V, op. cit., p. 736.
12. Binodini Dasi, *My Story and My Life as an Actress*, op. cit., p. 80.

AND THE STORY GOES ON

THERE CAN BE no conclusion to the story of the actress, only certain thoughts. Her story goes on from generation to generation with a few changes here and there. It is undeniable that the very fact the story has no ending is due to the courage of some women who for different reasons accepted the challenge that came their way—focused on a very tough learning process and produced results no one dreamed that they were capable of producing. There is no doubt that it was a life of uncertainty that they were accepting, especially in the first few years when there was no great name they could look up to. What they thought or felt is mostly lost since they were not preserved in the written word, except for a microscopic minority. One has to gather pieces of scattered evidences and put together a plausible picture. Simone de Beauvoir wrote in *The Second Sex* that an actress was to both men and women an object 'on sale'. 'To show herself was to sell herself or at least put herself on sale. Very few women actually got success—money, power or independence through theatre. They were under worked, under paid, and governed by the rules, appetites and expectations of a male controlled society. Yet some of them achieved success and in their self realization they find self-fulfillment as women.'[1]

But even when one focuses on the actress as I have done throughout the book, I have kept one thing in mind—that the actress was never above society. She was always a part of it—from the time she came in to the theatre till she left it. In fact, when she left it, society forgot her very quickly, and even the most feted actresses remained in public memory only as long as they were performing. And she too was always aware of social censure whether she found her niche in acting, singing or dancing. Total liberation, mental or economic, was a dream which remained elusive in this phase at least.

In England, the appearance of professional women actors was associated with some larger symptoms of change—a questioning of authority in politics and religion, experiments in sexual freedom, the post-war shift in class barriers and increased social mobility, and the circulation of new ideas about money, philosophy, morality and education. Certain changes too were taking place in theatre. A break in theatrical development had occurred due to the closure of playhouses during the English Civil War which had dried up the supply of male actors who could act as girls. Also, a change in the architecture of the playhouses meant smaller structures, making for a closer association with the audience. The restoration of Stuart rule brought an entourage of aristocrats who had developed a taste for actresses in the Continent as well as scenery and spectacle.[2] Initially, these actresses were respectable and were even married, but it was better for theatre business and the actress to claim the reverse. As the aura of immorality lingered, the playhouses thrived. The actresses were faced with insurmountable problems—they were not ladies but they had to act like them, they had to be literate, to be able to read, understand and memorise scores of plays. They had to cope with the exigencies of the public as well as dramatists. They had to control the audience backstage and face violence—financial remuneration was not enough as compensation. But they achieved sexual freedom and limited women's liberation.[3]

This was a period of great change in Indian society as well ushered in by British rule in society and culture. Western education had brought forth a new generation of writers in Bengal while introducing new elements in the cultural scene, theatre being one of them. Unlike in England, where it took eighty-four years to bring the actress into public theatre, in Calcutta women joined the public stage only one year later.

Improvement in cultural life was considered the goal of many at the end of the nineteenth century since only then could an improvement in national life and character be achieved. Theatre could redeem the lives of not only those directly associated with the performance but also the audience. That was why the performance of quality plays and the improvement of infrastructure of the play houses as well as the quality of acting was stressed upon in the writing of the time. As Kshetra Nath Bhattacharjee wrote in the *Education Gazette*, '. . . the more such theatres are started, acting will be improved and dramas (will be) composed in competition. The present theatres have no female artists on the staff. This will be considered a defect and means will be sought to remedy this defect. Some of the prostitutes are trying to receive education. If a few of such educated women are secured happy consequences will outweigh any mischief done.'[4] This statement brings in a trend of thought prevalent in society even before 1873. This idea of improvement through culture was in the minds of the literati. Realizing the impact that theatre had on the minds of youth and realizing the inevitability of women from prostitute families joining middle-class youth on stage, some thought that the situation could be saved if these women were provided with education. Thus, immorality was considered to be the outcome of fear arising out of insecurity which might lead these women to attempt to use the theatre as a stepping-stone to procuring a protector 'babu' from among the rich young men who chose to squander their leisure and fortune in theatrical pursuits. If these women could be educated, then they would acquire a confidence arising out of an ability to learn to become great actresses and achieve a sense of material and mental security that perfection in acting and the power derived from the adulation of an adoring public would bring.

Professionalism on stage appeared to be an insurmountable hurdle to the women who came from very poor backgrounds. Their education was too basic compared to the literary standard of the script they had to memorise. In fact, the various teachers and mentors read the dialogues aloud and the actresses simply learnt by rote. Unfortunately, though most of the actresses, having passed through the difficult test of learning their parts, never stuck it out for very long and simply used the stage as a stepping-stone for a life of financial security under the wings of a rich patron. For most of them, art was less important than financial security and the fears of their past life and that of their mothers cast long shadows. The actress always retained her womanly qualities no matter how famous she became and as an example of how she made the theatre family her own, Binodini in her autobiography talks about Bhuni who saved the life of a fellow actor and preserved the epitome of womanhood—i.e. being a mother and the nourisher. Once when the troupe which she belonged to was on its way to a performance in Krishnanagar, some distance away from Calcutta, an actor called Umichand fell ill. There was no water to be found anywhere. Bhuni, who was breastfeeding her baby took milk out in a small container for the afflicted actor trying her best to save his life, but in vain. Metaphorically too, actresses tried to save a company through self-sacrifice by donating all their jewellery. This was in the case of Amarendranath's Minerva. He was trying to manage both Classic and Minerva in hope of increasing his profits, but soon realized that the burden of two theatres was too heavy. Minerva started suffering losses and in an effort to redeem his losses, Amarendranath went on a tour to Dhaka with Minerva, but recurring losses disrupted the group. There was no money left even to return to the city. Finally, the actresses sold their jewellery to collect funds to save the company and return home.[5]

Once an actress gained fame, she would be lured away from other theatrical groups in order to make another theatre solvent. When Classic fell on bad times when local Muslim groups would not allow the performance of *Satnam*, Minerva took advantage of the situation with a performance of *Samsar*, which was an amalgam of different plays. Though some of the audience from Classic was diverted to Minerva, still the play was not really taking off. In that situation the only other way left was to bring in popular actors and actresses. So Tarasundari was brought in from Unique and Ardhendusekhar from Star.

The tantrums of established actresses were an expression of the realization of the special power that fame brought. Aparesh Chandra Mukhopadhyay recalls that when he was in his first role in Minerva as Probir in *Jana*, the established actress Tinkadi was offended since she had not been informed that she would be performing with a new and unknown actor Aparesh instead of Chunilal Deb who was also the manager and lessee. She was so offended that she tried to force Chunibabu to succumb to her demands but failed. With poor grace she had to give in and perform with Aparesh.[6] On the other hand, experienced actresses often contributed to productions with questions and suggestions to improve standards. When a play was repeated in another group after a successful production in one theatre, changes had to be introduced to ensure success. When the end of *Pratapaditya* was changed by Ardhendusekhar, Tarasundari warned him that the changes might not be welcomed by the audience.[7] Sometimes, according to the calibre of the actresses, Girish Ghosh emphasised a particular character during the dramatisation of Bankim's plays. When Tarasundari acted as Ayesha, she was not the 'sub heroine' compared to Tilottama, but the main character. Binodini too was made to perform sometimes as Ayesha and sometimes as Tilottama. When Sukumari Dutta was Bimala, then the character came into focus through clever script and inspired acting. She recalls an impromptu farce prepared by Ardhendu Sekhar Mustafi and rehearsed in the interval and performed because the audience could not leave the hall due to heavy rains.

Binodini Dasi believed that in the initial phase, at least, all those associated with the theatre were more concerned with the pursuit of art than with business. First of all, it was because the pay was too little to sustain the interest of those who were commercially-minded and second, it was a challenge to support something new that had been started in the country.[8] There cannot be any doubt about the dedication of Binodini to art. She gives instances where her immersion in the play proved to be dangerous—one was when the actresses performing in the play *Sarojini* as Rajput ladies performing the jauhar sacrifice when their husbands were defeated, jumped into real flames which were to act as funeral pyres. There were no electric lights and on the stage some sheets of tin were placed and thin logs lit and placed on them. Binodini remembers that once she was so caught up in her performance as Promila that she did not notice that her hair and clothes had caught fire and it was the prompt action of her co-actor Upendra Mitra who was on-stage who saved her from serious burns.[9] On another occasion in Great National when Binodini was acting as Britannia and flying through space on the stage, the wire which kept her afloat suddenly broke and she fell on the stage precipitously to the great shock of her co-actor, Girish Ghosh. Binodini, despite being shaken and hurt, recovered immediately and saved the day by starting to speak her allotted dialogue. Binodini also recalls that in the performance of *Nala Damayanti* there was a scene where some actresses would rise up from lotuses in a pond and held precariously on the flowers as they emerged. This was practiced for long hours to perfection by director Girish Ghosh himself and was a very popular scene in the play. One evening, one of the performers was absent and Girish wanted Binodini to appear in her place. Binodini was petrified of hanging over the flower without any practice at all. But there was no question of defying her mentor's command. As luck would have it her long hair got entangled in the wire as it was slowly lifting her up. She could feel it tearing from the roots. Finally one of her co-actors had to cut off her beautiful hair to free her. Binodini was not only mortified with shame in front of a full house but also found the loss of her hair most distressing.[10]

Bankim Chandra Chattopadhyay whose novels made very popular adaptations on stage praised Sukumari's performance as Bimala and Girijaya in *Kopalkundala* as true to life even when it was performed without the script. Once, during a performance, the script could not be found and Girish Ghosh improvised on stage while the actors and actresses were such experts that they followed his cue impromptu. Bankim Chandra was most impressed. Sisir Kumar Bhaduri did not have a high opinion about the actresses of his time and called them *phajil* or frivolous, only exceptions were Tarasundari, Kusumkumari, Charushila and Prova. They performed with all their heart and had tremendous talent. In his words, the rest of the actresses had low grade talent—*poimaal.*[11] Tarasundari received accolades on her acting from many leading critics of the time. Hemendra Kumar Roy wrote that Tara rose far above all actresses in serious roles. Her co-actor Danibabu could never reach the same heights in acting. Her diction and voice quality were outstanding and she was equally good in melodrama or in realistic plays. There was, unlike other performers, a mixture of spontaneity and a carefully considered plan of action in her performances. Her creative genius made her performances as Ayesha and Razia unforgettable. The poet Satyendranath Dutta, serenaded her extraordinary talent with a poem in her honour.[12] When Girish Ghosh's play *Sirajuddaula* was proscribed, he had to be present at the police station every day between 7 a.m. and 2 p.m. Finally, with the help of Jaladhar Sen and Suresh Samajpati, changes were made in the script and at Minerva, Tarasundari acted as Johra. The play electrified the audience at a time when politically Bengal was in an uproar in protest against the Partition of Bengal. The audience shouted slogans of *Bande Mataram* during the performance and on the first night, a Muslim poet congratulated Girish saying that he had the blessings of the entire Muslim community. The earnings too were high and the play ran consecutively for twenty-five nights earning Rs. 700 per night. The earnings of *Durgeshnandini*, another novel by Bankim Chandra Chatterjee adapted in to a play by Girish Ghosh with Tara acting as Ayesha, also earned Rs. 948 on the first night.

With the coming of the actress into the public theatre, the aura of respectability of the theatre was destroyed, together with its exclusivity. What had been the domain of men from established families was now thrown open to anyone who could buy a ticket. Just as class barriers in the audience were removed, so too acting no longer remained the prerogative of men belonging to similar backgrounds. Now anyone could make acting their profession. Public theatre not only brought women to acting, many more came to the audience. With the staging of mythological plays, combining sentiments of heroism, devotion and love, women who had till then stayed away from the 'den of vices' now started coming in large numbers and theatre became a source of entertainment for the whole family.[13]

With the introduction of religious plays and actresses bringing in authenticity in lead roles though their melodious singing, theatre received a new certificate. As Sushil Mukherjee points out, the Press and the public applauded Binodini's performance of Nemai in *Chaitanyaleela* in 1884, and the 'much condemned public theatre, the supposed haunt of all the rejected elements of the society, the truant young men and fallen women, could also be a centre of religious teachings and preaching, knowledge and enlightenment, moral and spiritual welfare of common man. The *samkirtan* on stage sent a wave of enthusiasm among the Bengalis, both in the city and outside and women from respectable families who were still a little shy of the theatre began to come to Star.'[14] This received further confirmation when the great reformer Sri Ramkrishna was so moved by Binodini's performance that he fell into a trance and later visited the Green Room to bless her. Not only were theatre and theatrical performances raised from the stigma of derision and neglect, it was a great opportunity for actresses to claim liberation from their past profession and background. Unfortunately, even Binodini did not capitalise on these blessings and soon after left the stage to go into anonymity, exchanging the chance to create a new horizon for women to embrace retirement as a soon-forgotten legend.

After the performance of *Chaitanyaleela*, a comparison was made between the Star Theatre and the European stage by a Shambhu Charan Mukherjee, Editor of *Reis and Rayat*, through the idiom of the actress. He refers to the play as having distinctly profited the audience spiritually though healthy recreation. 'Let the morality mongers try a dose of the sublime morality of the *Chaitanyaleela* . . . the language is chaste throughout, the makeup . . . the attitude-bearing and conduct—all were unexceptionable. What a contrast to the bawdy suggestiveness of the European Stage! We wish European gentlemen would come and see how far acting may be effective without meretricious aids or the attraction of the naked female person. Probably the average playgoer will vote the Star theatre too insipidly proper. The difference is characteristic. The contrast between the sober, fully dressed Baijis of sober motions and the fidgety ballet girl with her insufficient or flesh coloured covering and her fidgety leaps and curvets is but a type of the contrast between the thorough respectability of the Hindu stage and the doubtful propriety of the European theatre.' This was also supported in the reply by Colonel Olcott in *The Native Theatre*, where he points out that though 'the poor girl who played Chaitanya may belong to the class of unfortunates . . .' she performed the part so well that she became the Saint personified. There was not a 'lewd gesture, not a sensual glance of the eye, not the slightest suggestion of animal desire like those which make up the attraction of nautches to their patrons'.

Almost all the critics of public theatre and all men associated with theatre and writing on it felt obliged to make some apology for being associated with the actresses 'fallen women'. While in the same breath they speak of the excellence of their performances and the intense dedication of these 'despised' women to better their art as well as the deep appreciation of well-established and respected men for inspiring actors, all articles and books begin with a regret that their family and societal associations had to be severed due to their love for the theatre and proximity to actresses. Devkumar Roychowdhury had to add a chapter called the 'Strong Moral Integrity: The Play of Light and Shadow' ('Naitik Bol—Alo Chhayar Khela') in the biography of Dwijendralal Roy to discuss the phase where Dwijendralal started associating with the public stage and writing successful plays. He had to prove that the moral strength of the writer overcame the lure of the actresses whom he helped train to perform in his plays.[15] Monomohon Goswami finds it very unfair that a young man who associates himself with the theatre not to 'mix' with 'fallen women' but to cherish their passion for the art is considered unacceptable in respectable society. After all, no respectable family would send their daughters to act in theatre, so where else would the theatrical groups bring actresses from? There are no kissing or hugging scenes whereas in all European theatres, a scene at the local bar was almost inevitable.[16]

Society could also be very cruel to women in its demand for respectability. Kiron Chandra Data, wrote a biography of Sukumari Dutta who went through so much trouble after she was married off so that she could become respectable and was then asked to leave the stage which had given her fame and status in exchange for penury as a 'respectable' married woman with a child. As if it was not enough, she was then abandoned by her husband who could not take the social ostracism for having married a 'fallen woman'. Alone with a daughter to feed, Sukumari went back to the stage for sustenance, and was enterprising enough to form a theatrical group as well as write a semi-autobiographical play. Yet her biographer described her decision to rejoin the stage as 'destroying all the hopes of her husband,'[18] a husband who shirked all his responsibility, abandoned his family and fled the country soon after he destroyed Sukumari's successful career. Yet the biographer felt sympathy for him and accused Sukumari of going against his wishes. The article had been written under the pen name of *Bisheshoggo* (The Specialist) in 1912 proving that even the biographical writer was not above societal bindings.

In *Abhinetar Atmakatha*, Bhupendranath Bangopadhyay tells the story of an actor who was shunned by society except his wife. Though he was able to be successful in his profession, his wife could never be happy because of society's criticism of his association with fallen women. Even though the actor was never close to any particular actress and for him acting was his passion as well as his profession, his beloved wife slowly declined and died. Even on the day of her death, he had to leave her bedside to perform in a play. The actor expresses his regret at society's hypocrisy since all his family members and friends regularly attended the theatre, yet tortured his wife mentally about his alleged moral decline.

In 1913, Basanta Kumar Ghosh, wrote in defense of the women in Bengali theatre that for excellence in theatrical performance, it was necessary to bring in women. This fact is not even denied by the social reformers who hold the theatre in such contempt. He feels that those who condemn the art simply because the actresses happen to come from not-so-respectable backgrounds are themselves guilty of poor taste. Why can not actresses be regarded simply as artists? After all, when the management takes over the life of an actress, they simply lose their backgrounds and the audience should only see them through the prism of their performance.[18] Besides, even the prostitute is human. When she joins the theatre, it is to start a new vocation. Once she becomes an actress to earn her living and works extremely hard to achieve success in her performance, she gets paid a salary by the management and no longer has to pursue her old profession. But society remains unforgiving towards her and ignores reality. In fact, there are instances where some so-called stalwarts of refined society try their best to lure established and successful actresses away from their profession. Basanta Kumar laments that though we ape the West in all matters, we never encourage husband-wife duos to perform on stage, though, as in Western theatre that would remove the taint from acting profession forever. Why cannot educated Bengali gentlemen patronise Bengali theatre when the King of England attends theatre there to encourage the actresses? After all even the sage Ramakrishna did not hesitate to shower the stage and its actress with his blessings after watching a moving performance![19]

Many critics associated the falling reputation of the theatre not with the participation of the actress but with the change in public taste, especially after the coming of the Parsi theatre from the 1920s. Calcutta had two Parsi theatres at this time—the Corinthian Stage at Dharamtolla street and the Alfred Stage at Harrison Road. Sisir Kumar Bhaduri, recognised as the most talented theatre personality after Girish Ghosh, made his debut at the Madan Theatre. Parsi theatre captured the public imagination with spectacular as well as trick scenes, gorgeous costumes, clever stage illusions, surprising fantasies as well as popular songs and dances. Theatre was totally commercialised catering to the popular taste with thrills and violence, sentimental excesses and loud rhetoric, low clowning and unbelievable extravaganza—all remote from real life. It became a show business par excellence.[20] Even before that, there were symptoms of taste changing. Monomohon Goswami wrote in 1910 in *Natya Mandir* that the audience no longer knew how to watch theatre. It was for that reason that the quality of theatre had deteriorated. Natural acting was no longer appreciated by the audience who wanted pomp and grandeur. Even the song-and-dance sequences were remote from reality. The critics who abhorred these incongruent sequences in theatre were in a minority while the bulk of the audience enjoyed extravaganzas which had no link to reality. This phenomenon he believed to be universal. Goswami recalled the story of a manager of a well-known theatre in England who was very concerned about the quality of his plays but was saddened to see the failing Box Office sales. He was ultimately forced to follow the trend of the time and introduce young and beautiful actresses whose appearances were more spectacular than their acting. But the profits of the theatre increased greatly. One day, the manager stood outside the theatre watching the favourable reactions of his audience and one of them congratulated him on the success of his theatre. The manager replied, 'My theatre my Lord! Rather you say my brothel. . . .'[21]

Some of the critics blame the audience for demanding songs and dances at the most inappropriate moments in the play. This shows the poor taste of the theatre-goers, they claim. This is evident when good plays do not attract a decent audience whereas farces with songs and dances galore always run to full houses. Basanta Kumar Ghosh writes that the dramatist Amritalal Bose openly announced that the audience is the buyer and that the theatre conducts business following the tastes and demands of the audience. The theatre can provide any kind of entertainment, but the audience has to want it. 'Why don't,' asks Basanta Kumar, 'the reformers who are so censorious about the theatre look in to the task of improving the taste of the audience and the theatrical production would, as a natural corollary, be improved. On the other hand the reticence and purity of the actress is rather praiseworthy. When the heads of the audience are turned by the sensuality, body language and humour of popular actresses and they show their appreciation by making obscene gestures, catcalls or throwing garlands at them, the actresses flinch in distaste and often crush the garlands under their feet. Isn't this enough proof of their chastity and dedication to their art?'[22]

Sisir Kumar Bhaduri acting under the Madan Theatre banner, was considered by critics as having brought back the glory of Bengali theatre, lost since the death of Girish Ghosh which frivolity and playing to the gallery under Amarendranath had further undermined. With Sisir Kumar's inimitable performance in *Raghubir* on 12 March 1922, the lament about the degenerate audience was no longer appropriate and many educated men like Rabindranath Tagore, Abanindranath Tagore, Sarat Chandra Chattopadhyay and Rakhal Das Banerjee were attracted to the theatre. A veritable 'jugantar' revolution occurred.[23] Dilip Kumar Roy spoke about the development of a new style which he called an 'artistic' style in the performance of Sisir Kumar and the actresses who trained under him and commented that 'God's plenty existed in him.'[24] But the clash with the Madan management occurred during the preparation of *Alamgir.* The manager did not like the idea of a 'poor king' in the play and ordered very rich and lavish sets to be created in place of the broken-down palace sets that Sisir Kumar had created as befitting a poor Zamindar King. Sisir felt that a non-Bengali management would never understand the nuances of a Bengali play and interference in acting and production would hamper the quality he wanted.[25] He therefore decided to quit Madan which continued with Nirmalendu Lahiri on a new stage. But the Alfred Theatre on Harrison Road was not a very suitable place to take families to watch theatre and soon Madan moved from theatre to films.

Ultimately, it is not the struggles that remain, but the memories of the good performances. These legendary actresses remained in the memory of their admirers and critics and will continue to do so as long as the memory of Bengali public theatre remains. It is not their disreputable past that people remembered but that they were 'goddesses' or 'saints' or as 'self sacrificing women' that society wanted to model their women. Some of them acquired titles like 'Prima Donna Nightingale' (Sushilabala), or 'Bengali Siddons' for Kironbala, etc. Some got rare accolades like Kiron whose obituary in *Rais and Rayat* read, 'The dead actress was a rare flower of her profession, another young genius who promised to burst before long in to full bloom and splendor. In so young an age, she betrayed extraordinary talents. She had to interpret Chaitanya, perhaps the most difficult Bengali dramatic character, and in her delineation of it she proved herself thoroughly deserving of the exalted lift, if not equal to her glorious predecessor. As Sarala, she might be said to have made her real debut, and as Sarala, it is enough to say she can never be forgotten, for even now at the mention of the picture, many a playgoer's eyes must glisten with a tear.'[26] Narisundari was so popular for the superb rendition of her songs that people came to listen to her even though there were other more famed artists in the plays. For example, in *Chandrasekhar*, it was to listen to the songs by the character Dalani Begum that the audience came despite the presence of Amritalal Bose, Tarasundari in Star or Sushilabala in Minerva.[27] Charushila received many accolades in the newspapers for her performances. *Nachghar* praised her for her singing and acting in *Abu Hossain* and for her portrayal of Natabar in *Hashnohana*. *Nachghar* also admired the way she was able to portray aristocratic pride in Siraji Begum in *Digvijay*, performed in 1928.[28]

With theatre becoming professional, those associated with it had to belong to the theatre full-scale and could hardly hold on to a primary profession and keep the theatre as a hobby. For the actress, of course, the same applied since most of them came from prostitute families which had no alternative source of income. Also, I believe that once they joined theatre continuing with their previous profession would be difficult since they were now the cynosure of all eyes and needed to maintain a certain aura of mystery as befitting a star as well as being credible in their role. The main objection, evident in the newspapers, in getting women from prostitute families as actresses to play the roles of chaste women and divine goddesses or even in men with divine characteristics was that of unsuitability as if they were in some way cheating the public. Actresses who had given up the profession that their mothers led were totally dependent on their salaries from the theatre for livelihood and for their future. This was because, unlike an actor who could continue acting for as long as he was alive, it was not so for an actress. In her old age, the roles that she would get were very limited and they would always be threatened by newer entrants who were willing to work for roles at much lower salaries. Also, their scope of then finding a protector would be minimal and the option of returning to the life of a prostitute after being feted by the public as a goddess was unthinkable.

The final question that one may ask is what makes one actress more acceptable than others. In the end, the acceptability of an actress and her longevity depends on many factors. First of all was her performing capability preserved in people's memories—when an actress is remembered by a writer it preserves her memory. Of course, sometimes certain aspects of her talent get highlighted more than others according to the taste of the person appreciating her, but it generally makes for remembrance. Added to this would be her ideas if they were expressed anywhere. Binodini is remembered more than all the other actresses not only because of her immense talent and her pioneering status, but more so because she fulfilled all the criteria of mythmaking. She was blessed by a living saint, Sri Ramakrishna, she was trained, mentored and later made into an iconic figure by the greatest theatre personality in Bengal, Girish Chandra Ghosh. Finally, the greatest quality of an idol—she withdrew from the limelight at the height of her glory. She never let anyone see or imagine her decline—neither on stage nor in physical appearance. For the generations to come she remained not just an actress, but a pioneer who opened the door for thousands of women to stand before the stage lights, a path-breaking authoress writing at a time when women remained behind the veil, neither seen nor heard.

The other actresses who stayed green in public memory were also those who were able to keep in print their talent, either directly or through other authors. The reviews, memoirs and biographies written on these women became vital testimonies without which even the greatest performances would have slipped away from public memory.

The poems of Tarasundari and the drama *Apurba Sati* of Sukumari Datta refresh our memory all the time. In fact the case of Golaap, or Sukumari Datta there is a point to be noted. Her achievements (though based on testimony of others as she did not write her autobiography) were considerable and significant. She was not only one of the first actresses on stage, but her name-change was due to her popularity in a stage play. But any memory about her is connected more to her personal life and her failed marriage. Yet it is her struggle to overcome odds which make her story so inspirational. She had been forced to give up theatre when she was to give birth to her child, but when she was abandoned by her spineless husband, she decided to take up her destiny in her own hands. She formed her own theatrical group, a first by a woman, a training camp (another first) she then wrote a play (another first by a woman) which was to be performed before women only (again a first testified to in her own words). But Sukumari never attained iconic status possibly because she had no strong voice championing her cause. Tarasundari on the contrary did, and if she was not very successful in the choice of patron or lover, the first time since Amarendranath was too engrossed in and tormented by his own achievements to champion another, in her second choice was lucky, and Aparesh Chandra Mukhopadhyay documented Tara's achievements in a mature and detached manner in his autobiography *Rangalaye Trish Bochhor.*

The second reason is her own voice. Whereever any writing exists on what an actress thought or did, it is far more effective than any biography. What Binodini Dasi left through her writing was even greater than what she did through her acting. For women of that age and the ages that have followed, she remained a shining example of what a woman can achieve despite the disadvantages of birth. She not only inspired many more actresses but also lots of women to write as well. No actress in India is better known than Binodini Dasi as a pioneer both in acting and writing. It is true that another prostitute, Nabin Kali Debi, had before her written a book called *Kamini Kalanka*[29] in 1870 but *Amar Kotha, Amar Natyajiboner Arambha* (*My Story* and *My Life as an Actress*) and two books on poetry (*Basana* and *Kanak O Nalini*) by a professional actress who inspired the writing of many plays, was a brilliant performer in male and female roles, a competent singer as well and achieved the crowning glory of being blessed by the living saint of the day Sri Ramkrishna Paramhansa, was indeed a final and glorious curtain call. It is no wonder that her autobiography would, as Girish Ghosh predicted, inspire many other women to rise above their station through the medium of art. In my eyes, what made Binodini truly great as is evident from her own writing is that every sacrifice she made for art and her own conscience, she made consciously and willingly. She had the whole fraternity of actors including her mentor Girish Ghosh at her mercy when they were thrown out of their theatre and were dependent on Binodini to sell herself to create a new one. Perhaps no one ever considered the immense sacrifice she made when she compromised with her own dreams of true love and put herself up to the highest bidder.

We find the other actresses scattered in many memoirs and writings on theatre in contemporary Bengali journals. When one constructs shadowy pictures of some of them through all the evidence available, some surprise us by presenting themselves as strong, positive and creative women whom time has forgotten. Also, public memory has its own stereotypical prism through which it remembers women achievers. It is very rarely that we would like to remember strong, defiant women who survived through their own mettle, who did not need to be protected, but in fact gave support and protection to others—be it their mentors or patrons (Tinkadi to Girish Ghosh, Sushilabala to Narendranath, Prova to Sisir Bhaduri), husbands (Kankaboti to Sisir Bhaduri) and daughters (Sukumari). But that will be another story.

Notes

1. Simone de Beauvoir, *The Second Sex*, London: Vintage Books, p. 711.
2. Richard Findlater, *The Player Queens*, London: Weidenfeld and Nicolson, 1976.
3. Ibid.
4. Kshetranath Bhattacharjee, *Education Gazette*, quoted in H.N. Dasgupta, *The Indian Theatre*, vol. 1, Delhi: Gyan Publishing House, 1009.
5. Aparesh Ch. Mukhopadhyay, *Rangalaye Trish Bochhor*, Kolkata.
6. Ibid., p. 45.
7. Ibid., p. 50.
8. Binodini Dasi, 'Amar Abhinetri Jiban', in *Amar Kotha O Onyanyo Rochona*, ed. Soumitra Chattopadhyay and Nirmalya Acharya, new edn., Calcutta, 1987, p. 97.
9. Ibid., p. 102.
10. Ibid., p. 104.
11. Shankar Bhattacharya, *Natyacharya Sisirkumar*, Calcutta: D.M. Library, 1970, pp. 124–5.
12. Ibid., p. 125.

13. Sushil Kumar Mukherjee, *The Story of Calcutta Theatres, 1753–1980*, Calcutta: K.P. Bagchi, 1982, p. 52.
14. Ibid., p. 66.
16. Devkumar Roychowdhury, *Dwijendralal: A Life*, Calcutta: Adhyayan, 2nd edn., 1964, pp. 270–308.
16. Monomohon Goswami, 'Rangabhumi Bhalobashilam Keno', in *Shotabdir Natya Chinta*, op. cit., p. 115.
17. Kiron Chandra Datta, *Suprasidhha Abhinetri*, Sukumari Datta, *Shotabdir Natya Chinta*, op. cit., p. 132.
18. Basanta Kumar Ghosh, 'Ranganari O Rangabhumi', in *Shatabdir Natyachinta*, op. cit., p. 168.
19. Ibid., pp. 169–71.
20. Sushil Kumar Mukherjee, *The Story of Calcutta Theatres*, op. cit., p. 522.
21. Monomohon Goswami, op. cit., p. 107.
22. Basanta Kumar Ghosh, op. cit., p. 169.
23. Moni Bagchi quoted in Sankar Bhattacharya, *Natyacharya Sisirkumar*, op. cit., p. 78.
24. Ibid., pp. 74–5.
25. Ibid., p. 97.
26. Debnarayan Gupta, *Banglar Nat Nati*, vol. I, Calcutta: Sahitya Lok, 1985, p. 127.
27. Ramapati Dutta, *Rangalaye Amarendranath*, ed. Debjit Bandopadhyay, Kolkata: Dey's Publishing, 2004.
28. Debnarayan Gupta, op. cit., pp. 25–6.
29. Nabin Kali Debi, *Kamini Kalongko*, First published in 1277 BS (1870), ed. Sumanta Banerjee, Kolkata: Wild Strawberries Books, 2010.

SHORT BIOGRAPHICAL SKETCHES

Golaap Sundari, later Sukumari Dutta: Performance (1873–81?)

One of the first four actresses to join Bengal Theatre, Golaap lived with her mother, near Mahesh. A beautiful actress, with a melodious voice, she acted in a number of productions in Bengal Theatre before moving on to Great National Theatre under the aegis of Upendranath Das who wanted to bring about social reforms through the theatre. On 2 January 1875, Golaap acted in *Sarat Sarojini* where her character's name was Sukumari. The play was a great success and Golaap's popularity as Sukumari was such that the name stuck. In fact, she herself used it as an author in her drama *Apurba Sati*.

Upendranath's dream was to remove the stigma that hung over theatre and those associated with it. He thought that if the actors and actresses could be married then the theatre would win a good name for itself and actresses would no longer be considered as polluting the good name of theatre. He arranged for the marriage of Sukumari to Goshtobehari Dutta, a young actor from a well-to-do family who was dependent on Upendranath. They were married by the Marriage Act III of 1872. But the step was not a happy one for the young people. A debate raged in the newspapers and the boy's family refused to be associated with Goshtho. Surviving on a lean income, he and Sukumari lived in penury in a slum as Sukumari had left the theatre in order to reinforce their 'respectable' life through motherhood. A short while later they had a daughter. Unable to cope with the social seclusion he was faced with once his patron and friend Upendranath Das left the country for health reasons, Goshtho abandoned his wife and daughter and followed Das to England. To tide over the financial crisis Sukumari first started a training camp and then wrote a play *Apurba Sati* which was staged at Great National Theatre on 23 August 1875. It was also performed in Bengal Theatre. Sukumari was possibly the first woman dramatist. She also became the first woman to form her own theatrical group with the help of Ashubabu, a youth of Bhavanipur, though the group did not last long. As critics point out, when all these efforts failed, Sukumari in desperation resumed her old profession. She joined Star where under Girish Ghosh's direction she performed as Motibibi in *Kopalkundala*, as Suryamukhi in *Bishabriksha*, as Rohini in *Krishnakanter Will* (all adaptations of the great novelist Bankim Chandra's works) and won great acclaim. Towards the end of her career, Sukumari joined Classic under Amarendranath and was able to hold her own against young actresses. However, she retired from public theatre due to ill health. In her long stage life of almost 28 years Golaap acted in Bengal, Great National, Emerald, Classic, Star and Arora Theatres.

In 1875, Golaap wrote *Apurba Sati* under the name by which she was more popularly known—Sukumari Dutta. *Apurba Sati* was reprinted in 1882. Dedicated to Maharani Swarnamoyee Devi, the book bore some distinct marks. For instance, it was surprising that more than once Latin was used in the headings of the work (Apruba Sati-Castus Mirabillis and instead of 'Preface' the word 'Pro-video' is used). In her introductory words, she writes that she was presenting the play before Bengali women before it is placed before the general public: 'If in our varied mirrors my sisters do not see their colourful faces, then will my incomparable hope regarding mirrors be lost in the future hollows of time.' Here there is mention of Ashutosh Das as one of the writers. Thus, it is possible to suppose that the use of ornamental literary Bengali and that of Latin words were his contribution. The drama comprises two poems and 11 songs, many of them set to various Hindusthani classical *ragas* and varied *taals*.

Jagattarini: Performance (1873–1904)

Though four actresses were hired by Bengal Theatre, only two of them took part in the 1873 *Sharmistha* performance. Jagattarini was one of them. There were mixed reactions in the contemporary press about her performance in *Sharmistha*, but in the next play *Ubhoy Sankat*, which was a farce by Ramnarayan Tarkaratna, Jagattarini creditably acquitted herself. Thereafter, in *Mohanter ei ki kaaj*, which took the city by storm

Jagattarini acted as the clever conniving second wife Mandakini. In *Durgeshnandini,* she was Tilottama. She then shifted to Great National and quite understandably her name doesn't always appear in the advertisements since there was stiff competition to be faced from the popular stars of the time. In 1889, Jagattarini joined the Bina Theatre and stayed on when it became Indian Theatre/City Theatre to join in performances of *Lakkyaheera*, *Ghosher Po*, *Chaturali*, *Tatka-Totka*, *Sarala*, *Tajjyab Byapar*, *Bilwamangal*, *Bibaha Bibhrat*, etc. In 1889, Jagattarini performed under Girish Ghosh's direction in Star in plays like *Prafulla* (Jagamoni), *Belick Bazar*, *Bibaha Bibhrat*, *Chorer opor Batpari*, and *Haranidhi* (Haimabati). After these, Jagattarini followed Ghosh to Minerva where she performed as Bhabatarini and Bridhha in the farce *Sabyatar Pnara*. In *Karametibai,* she received praise as Krittika, and in *Panch Kone* as Matangini. In *Prafulla*, her characterization of Jagamoni was in competition with that of Star's *Prafull*a and according to most critics her performance had improved.After Ghosh left Minerva for Star, Jagattarini was not noticed much in the advertisements and only comes back in circulation after joining Classic under Amarendranath who brought Ghosh as director. In 1901, Jagattarini is seen as performing as Durga in competition with Arora. In 1902, she was Ramenswari in *Aayna*. She also performed in *Hariraj* and *Vikramaditya* in Classic even after Ghosh left and performed as Annapurna in Rabindranath's *Chokher Bali* and Lakshmi in Shivratri. Her last performance possibly took place around 1904.

ELOKESHI: PERFORMANCE (1873–98)

Elokeshi had previous experience in performing in Jatras and was one of the first four actresses to be inducted by Bengal Theatre. Only two of them were ready for performance in *Sharmistha* in 1873 and Elokeshi performed as Debjani. She then took part in all the plays staged in the next few years in Bengal Theatre. She performed as Ashmani in *Durgeshnandini*, as Kulsum in *Chandrasekhar*. Then she moved to Star and performed as Maheswari in *Molina Bikhash* under Girish Ghosh's direction. She passed away in 1898.

SHYAMASUNDARI: PERFORMANCE (1873–)

Shyamasundari was one of the four actresses chosen by Bengal Theatre for introducing actresses into Bengali public theatre, as advised by Michael Madhusudan Dutta. She performed in *Mayakanan*, *Swapnadhan*,

Bidyasundar, and *Jemon Karma Temni Phal*. Though her career was neither very successful nor very long, she will always remain in public memory as one of the pioneers of the stage.

Binodini Dasi (1863–1941): Performance (1874–86)

Binodini was married in her childhood but was never taken to her husband's home. Sri Purnachandra Mukhopadhyay and Brajanath Seth who belonged to Great National Theatre would visit the house she stayed in to attend musical soirees of another singer who lived there. Binodini's mother sent her along with Mukhopadhyay and Seth to Great National Theatre in the hope that she would at least be fed and clothed. Her first role was that of a maid in *Benisamhar*. She recalls in her autobiographical *Amar Abhinetri Jibon* how nervous she was on her first night and how she kept forgetting her lines and was tempted to run away rather than face the audience. However, Binodini successfully performed her part and her very nervousness was appropriate for her role. The first stage manager of Bengal at Great National Theatre, Dharmadas Sur's approval was her true inspiration. Her next performance was as the heroine in *Hemlata*. She was a young girl but had to be dressed as a young woman and perform as one. She claimed that her success was due not to her talent but the brilliant training of her mentors Dharmadas and Radhamadhab Kar and the then doyen of Bengali Theatre Girish Ghosh who made her the household name she became. She acted in many operas like *Sati ki Kalankini*, *Adarsha Sati*, *Kanak Kanan*, *Anandaleela*, *Kaminikunja* and farces like *Sadhabar Ekadashi*, *Kinchit Jalajog*, *Chorer opor Batpari*, etc. She was part of the world of theatre for twelve years and retired from acting when she was at the pinnacle of her glory in 1886. Even more than her acting, the reason why she has stayed a legend is because her performance in *Chaitanya Leela* got the blessings of the sage Sri Ramkrishna. During her years on the stage, she acted in 90 roles in 80 plays. She successfully portrayed different roles like Sita, Pramila, Draupadi, Radhika, Kaikeyi, Uttara, Damayanti, Gopa, Satyabhama, Chintamoni in mythological plays and Kanchan, Kamini, Ayesha, Tilottama, Ashmani, Manorama, Kopalkundala, Motibibi, Kundanandini, Bilashini, Rangini, etc., in historical and social plays. In an age when women performing in roles for women was revolutionary, Binodini went a step further—performing in male roles with élan, like that of Chaitanya. She performed six roles in a single play *Meghnad Badh*. She has been praised by intellectuals like Bankim Chandra, Edwin Arnold and Colonel Olcott, and was the darling of the contemporary journals and newspapers. She was associated with four theatres in her career as an actress: Great National (December 1874–April 1876), Bengal Theatre (April 1876–August 1877), National Theatre (December 1877-Febuary 1883) and Star which was built in her honour though Girish Ghosh refused to allow it to be named as Binodini Theatre as had been suggested (July 1883–January 1887). She retired from acting at the age of 23 and died on 12 Febuary 1941, in loneliness and penury. She had a daughter by her patron with whom she spent a part of her life in anonymity but lost her at a young age of thirteen.

Binodini has remained alive in people's mind even when she retired from the limelight as a writer. She wrote in *Natyamandir* and *Rup O Ranga* but both serialized writings remained incomplete. Twenty-six years after her retirement she wrote her autobiography *Amar Jibon*, volume I in 1912. In *Rup O Ranga*, *Amar Abhinetri Jiban* was published in 1924 in eleven parts but was stopped abruptly. (12 Samkhya 4 Magh 1331 BS to 28 Samkhya, 26 Baishakh, 1332 BS.; 33 years after she quit the stage.) *Basana*, a book of poems was published in 1896 (41 poems in 84 pages) dedicated to her mother. In 1905, *Kanak O Nalini* was published as a verse-novel dedicated to her late thirteen-year-old daughter Shakuntala Dasi.

KADAMBINI: PERFORMANCE (1874–88)

An expert at singing and dancing, Kadambini entered Great National Theatre through Madan Mohon Burman and performed in *Ananda Kanan* as Leela the maid. Later, with Burman she left Great National and joined Bengal Theatre. She stayed there only for two months but made her mark in a number of plays. She joined Dharmadas Sur's troupe for the tour of north India from which she returned in 1875. Soon after, Madan Mohon and Kadambini joined Upendranath Das in Aryan Theatre which specialized in performing patriotic plays. Finally Girish Ghosh inducted her in to the newly-established National Theatre in 1877, and she got the role of Mandodari in Michael Madhusudan's *Meghnad Badh* and Rani Bhawani's role in *Palashir Yuddha*. In Girish's

Agomoni, Kadambini performed as Menoka to Binodini's Uma. There her claim to fame was to introduce Agomoni songs in theatre. (These are songs sung to usher in Durga Puja. The Agomoni songs are sung by Menoka, the mother of Durga who pleads with her husband to fetch their daughter back from her husband's home.) She was also successful in another opera *Akal Bodhon*. In *Anilanda Man* (1878), she performed the role of Damayanti; in *Mrinalini* she was Girijaya and in *Bisha Briksha* she was Suryamukhi. She was also successful in opera plays like *Alibaba O Challish Chor*, *Promode Kanan*, *Paristhan* and *Kamini Kunja*. In 1880, when Girish became manager of National Theatre, Kadambini took part in many memorable roles: Kusum in *Mohini*, Mandodari in *Ravana Badh*, Sita in *Sitar Bonobash*, Kaushalya in *Ramer Bonobash* and Sudeshna in *Pandaber Ogyatobash*. In 1883, Pratap Johuri tried to cut theatre expenses by reducing the salaries of the actresses. In protest, Girish left National followed by many actors and actresses. Star opened in 1883 and Kadambini performed as Prosuti in *Dakshayajna* and Suniti in *Dhruva Charitra*. Soon after, she went in to oblivion and re-emerged in 1888 at the new Star in Biraja's role in *Nasiram* and as Pramada in *Sarala*.

Jadumoni: Performance (1874–)

Jadumoni started as a Baiji singing mujras in musical soirees. Then Bhuvanmohon Niyogi approached her to join the new stage of Great National Theatre. A fire had stopped performances in Great National Theatre, which initially refused to take actresses. Meanwhile, actresses were already performing in Bengal Theatre successfully. The reconstructed Great National realized that it would be unrealistic to refuse to employ actresses. Along with Jadumoni came Kshetramoni, Rajkumari, Haridasi, and Kadambini who were the other set of pioneering actresses. Jadumoni's roles in the Great National were Radhika in *Sati ki Kalankini*, and various roles in *Purubikram*, *Bharate Yavan*, and *Rudrapal*—all in 1874. She was most successful in the opera-style plays where she could sing. After *Anandakanan* internal problems started in Great National and along with others, Jadumoni left to join Bengal Theatre. Although her singing made her very popular, she could not stay there. She rejoined Great National but when some actors and actresses were taken by Dharmadas Sur to tour north and west India, Jadumoni stayed back and under the direction of Mahendralal

Bose performed in a number of plays in Great National. The plays included *Shadhabar Ekadashi*, *Noysho Rupeya*, *Tilottama Sambhav*, *Sakshat Darshan*, and *Nandan Kanan*. Her singing of Bharat Sangeet in *Padmini* won her great praise. Jadumoni stayed steadfast to her loyalty for Bhuban Chandra Niyogi when Dharmadas Sur refused to help the former financially and left with numerous actors and actresses. In *Sarat Sarojini*, Jadumoni's singing received special mention in the staging of *Englishman* on 17 August. She was the leading lady of the next few plays: *Nildarpan*, *Daktarbabu*, *Kanakpadma* and, *Brittasamhar*, but when Upendranath Das became Director and Amritalal Bose was Manager, Jadumoni had to make way for other actresses.

Kshetramoni: Performance (1874–1910)

After joining Great National she performed in *Sati ki Kalankini* as Brinda, in *Purubikram* as Oindrila (as a rival to Oindrilla by Golapsundari in Bengal), in *Ananda Kanan* as Ahamika, a serious character and in *Chorer Opor Batpari* as Ginni, a comic role. In *Sarat Sarojini* and *Nildarpan*, Kshetramoni acted before she joined the group of performers who left for the tour of north India with Dharmadas Sur. They returned in May 1875. In Amritalal's farce *Chorer Opor Batpari*, she performed as Ginni opposite Amritalal. In the next few plays, she had bit roles till a farce *Gajadananda* which satirized the presence of the Prince Edward in the inner sanctum of High Court Lawyer Jagadananda Mukhopadhyay's home was started, where she had the leading role. The farce was considered an insult to the British prince and the performance was forbidden. Close to ten artists were arrested and the Dramatics Control Act was passed on 29 February 1876. Later, in the productions of National Theatre under Girish Ghosh, all roles of female demons in mythological plays were performed by Kshetramoni. In 1881, in *Ravana Badh*, Kshetramoni was dressed as Durga. Dharmadas Sur, the manager wanted to surprise the audience and so ordered eight hands made of clay to be made to fit her. Kshetramoni was dressed up in jewels and weapon as befitting the warrior goddess. She had to endure the weight of the dress for almost half an hour every night and would eventually faint in exhaustion. Girish Ghosh was angered since he had asked for the hands to be made of tin so that they would be light. The incident, however, proved Kshetramoni 's patience and mettle. She was also brilliant as Aladdin's mother in *Aladdin* and Nikasha in

Sitar Banabash. When Girish Ghosh left National Theatre in 1883, Kshetramoni followed him. In *Dakhhayajna* in Star, Kshetramoni was Tapasvini in 1883 and in *Chaitanya Leela* she was Moha in 1884. In *Bibaha Bibhrat*, her characterization of the maid was considered splendid. She was Malini and Gopini in *Nimai Sanyas*, and in 1885 in *Budhhadev Charita*, she acted as three characters. In 1886, in *Bilwamangal* too, Kshetramoni was again a maid Thako. After a gap, she was back in Emerald Theatre as Sohagi in *Bishad* in 1888. After a few performances in old plays, Kshetramoni was seen in 1903 as Savitri in *Nil Darpan* in Star and in 1904, and as Milkman's wife in *Pratapaditya*. She stayed until 1909–10 in Star but performed in old roles.

Basanta Kumari: Performance (1877–1921)

The sister of the more successful Bhusan Kumari, Basanta however joined theatre six years before her. Basanta Kumari joined Great National in 1877 with a minor role in *Meghnad Badh*. But she performed in chorus parts for a long time until 1897, when she got the role of Begum in *Abu Hossain* in Minerva. In the same year, she was Phulwali in *Hirak Jubilee* and Mandakini in *Mayabashan* at Star. In 1900, in Minerva she got two roles of Rohini and Lolita, in the opera *Nandadulal*. She sang three songs and her *kirtans* earned her much fame. In *Bisha Briksha*, she was Heera but the play stopped after twelve nights. In Star it was Dwijendralal Roy's play *Rana Pratap* that brought Basanta Kumari in to the limelight as Daulatunnissa. Her beautiful face and melodious voice cast a spell over the audience. But her competition was against a powerful co-star Narisundari in Star while there was the danger of successful performances of the duo Tarasundari and Sushilabala in Minerva in the same play. It was Basanta Kumari's Tappa-style songs that inspired the audience to shout repeated encores. In *Tarubal*, she performed as Parul, in *Pratapaditya* as Kalyani, in *Sabitri* as Alikshara and in *Laila Majnu* as Motiya. In 1906, in *Palashir Prayaschitta*, she was Lutfunnissa and in *Chandrasekhar* Basanta was Kulsum. In 1908, she acted in *Prafulla* as Gyanada, in *Phatik Jol* as Phulia, in *Nasiram* as Sona, in *Jadukari* as Tarita, in *Kamini Kanchan* as Amiya, in *Bilwamangal* as Ahalya and in *Indira* as Phullara.

In 1909, Basanta acted in *Kusume Keet* as Chitra, in Ashalata as Julia and in *Rajsimha* in 1910 as Jebunnissa. In *Dasha Chakra* she was Subala and in *Daksh Yajna* she was Tapaswini and in *Behula* in the title role. In 1911, National Theatre closed its doors and Great National opened with Rabindranath Tagore's Dalia adapted as *Jibone Morone*. Basanta Kumari was Dalia though she was overshadowed in this play by Sushilabala. She returned to Star in the same year and there she performed in two plays. In 1912, when the doyen of Bengali theatre, Girish Ghosh passed away, along with many others Basanta Kumari too was devastated. She then played an important part in the memorial service for Girish Ghosh to ensure that the actresses were represented, since all the actresses to whom Girish had been a messiah and mentor wanted to be able to pay their respects openly. In her speech, she spoke of how she considered herself fortunate that she, an actress from a downtrodden section of society, was allowed to express her grief to the public. 'Actresses', she said, 'were considered to belong to no one'. '. . . [they] have the greatest respect and have learnt the art of acting at his [Girish's] feet but much more than that he touched their hearts, treated them like daughters and sprinkled the waters of peace and hope on the burnt embers of their degraded lives.'

She stayed with Star until 1915 and performed in various plays. The lure of a higher salary brought her to Monomohon Theatre where she performed as Helen in *Chandragupta*. She stayed in that theatre till 1920.

GANGAMONI: PERFORMANCE (1881–)

Ganga Bai was an established singer who came to stay as boarder in Binodini's grandmother's house. She had become friends with the young girl Binodini whom she taught singing. It was Ganga Bai who asked Sri Purnachandra Mukhopadhyay and Brajanath Seth associated with Great National Theatre, who used to visit her to listen to her music, to take Binodini to the Great National Theatre to become an actress. She herself joined National Theatre much later because she was illiterate and a basic knowledge of reading and writing in Bengali was essential for an actress to learn their parts. In 1881, when she finally joined she got the role of Subhadra in *Abhimanyubadh* under the training of Girish Ghosh. In 1882, she acted as Guhak's wife in *Ramer Banabash* and Mandodari in *Sitaharan*. She was Baruna in *Molin Mala*, which was an opera and so needed her musical expertise. In 1883, in the new Star Theatre, Gangamoni acted as Bhrigu's wife in *Daksha Yajna* and Rajmata in *Nala Damayanti*. They were both small roles. In

Kamale Kamini in 1884, she performed as Lahana and Girish put her musical talent to full use in *Srivatsa Chinta* where Gangamoni sang 21 songs. In the historic *Chaitanya Leela* where Binodini was blessed by Sri Ramkrishna for her performance as Chaitanya, Gangamoni was her constant support as Sachimata. In 1885, in *Prabhas Yajna* she was Yashoda and sang in the *kirtan* style. In 1886, in *Bilwamangal*, she was Pagolini, which was later performed as challenging roles by other great actresses like Tinkari, Narisundari and, Sushilabala. Gangamoni stayed in Star even after Binodini left and in Star's new stage, Gangamoni acted as Sona in *Nasiram*. On 31 December 1895, the *Statesman* reported that the rendering of the character of Sona was 'superb' and that she was 'one of the warmest favourites of the audience'. Not content to be just a singing star, Gangamoni also 'acted' in *Sarala* as Shyama Dasi and in *Haranidhi* as Kadambini, in *Naramedha Yajna* as Katyayani and *Bijay Basanta* as Shanta. She also acted and sang in a Hindi play *Ramasvamedha*. In 1896, when she performed in Girish Ghosh's *Kalapahar*, she sang classical songs on stage but her name was printed in the advertisements thereafter as Ganga Baiji.

Harisundari: Performance (1882–1934)

Harisundari was also known as Blackie. Her long performance reign started with Girish Ghosh and ended in Sisir's time. She began as Bhramar of *Krishnakanter Will* in Emerald Theatre. In 1894, she joined Minerva. At that time, Girish was the dramatic director at Minerva and Harisundari received training under him. She acted as Kumudini in *Sabyatar Phanra* in 1894 and as Bedeni in *Phonir Moni* in 1896. Then she joined Classic where Amarendranath gave her the chance to perform in many roles. It was quickly noted that whichever theatre Amarendranath joined, Harisundari followed him there. Whether in Classic or Minerva, in New Classic or Grand Theatre, Harisundari was always by his side. She also had great talent in singing and playing instrumental music, besides being an expert in playing the table organ and piano.

Bhushankumari: Performance (1883–)

Bhushankumari was a skilled singer and dancer and as Sita performed creditably in *Ramer Banabash*. In Sitaharan, she was Sagar's wife and in *Pandaber Ogyatobash*, she was Uttara. Thus, when Girish started *Dhruva Charitra*, on the advice of the actress Kadambini, Bhushan Kumari was chosen as the young boy Dhruva and excelled as a boy. After that she did a couple of performances as a girl in *Nala Damayanti* (Sunanda) where her songs too were memorable and in the 'grand spectacle' of *Kamale Kamini* which boasted 'scenes, mechanism and scientific appliances', she was Sushila. In 1884, she again performed as a young boy in *Brishaketu*. In *Hirar Phul*, she showed her expertise in dance as well, as Rati under the training of Kashinath Chattopadhyay. The songs of the play became very popular. She was equally good in the roles of Bhadra in *Srivatsa Chinta* and Bishnupriya in *Nimai Sanyas*. Her songs as Devabala in *Buddhacharit* in 1885, were so spiritual that they became Narendra Nath Dutta (Swami Vivekananda)'s favourites. The exact opposite portrayal as a Khemtawali in *Bellick Bazar* proved her mettle as a performer. In 1887, in *Rup Sanatan*, Bhushan acted as a Hindi-speaking boy with lines in a particular dialect difficult to emulate. In 1889, Girish directed his play *Prafulla* where Bhushan was given the title role. She then followed Girish to Minerva where she performed as Radhika in *Saptamite Bisharjan*, a farce. In *Jana*, she performed as Madanmanjari and then in 1894 as Bela in *Swapner Phool*. In the operatic play *Phonir Moni*, Bhushan played the role of Baari.

Bhushan Kumari joined Classic in 1897 and in *Alibaba* she was Sakina. In 1897, on Christmas Day, Bhushan acted in two roles: Shashikala and Shyekrani in Amarendranath's *Kajer Khatam*. When in 1898, Amarendranath started his *Dol Leela*, Bhushan was Sri Radha. After this when plague struck Calcutta and the theatre was deserted Girish took some actors and actresses outside the city. Bhushan went with him as part of Marvel Theatre but it did not run. When Girish Ghosh returned to Classic, Bhushan did not get a chance since Classic had already taken up the services of Tinkadi and Pramadasundari. Some months later Bhushan got a chance in Classic to perform Phullara in *Indira*. Though she was missed out on some plays, thereafter Bhushan was chosen for the opera *Deldar* and as Dhara she had six songs to sing followed by *Karametibai* where she again performed as Radhika. In *Srikrishna* Bhushan was given the role of Radha. Though it was a controversial role due to historical fallacies, yet it was considered justified since the character sang songs in a particularly spiritual manner. Her last important role was Jayanti in *Sitaram* and after that her name does not seem to come up in the advertisements.

Tarasundari (1878/9–1948): Performance (1884–1933)

Though born in an obscure locality Tarasundari rose to great heights in public theatre by sheer merit despite remaining in the shadow of more famous stars. Her mother brought Tara and her sister Nrityakali up in abject poverty—a time that left a deep impact on Tara's mind. Tara's mother knew Binodini's mother quite well. Binodini, who was already an established actress at the time, took the young child Tarasundari to Star Theatre quite often. For a long time Tara could not get a good role though she acted a few times in the role of a young boy in *Chaitanya Leela.* Soon after, Gopal Sil bought the building that housed Star Theatre. Sil planned to renovate it and start a new theatre called Emerald. Star Theatre bought a plot of land in Hatibagan and started the construction of a theatre. During the construction, the theatrical party left for performances in Dacca and around this time Binodini left Star—a move which severed Tara's connection with theatre as well.

In 1888, when Star completed the theatre building the company returned to Calcutta and began rehearsals of Girish Ghosh's play *Nasiram.* Neelmadhab, the main actor wanted Tarasundari back in Star. Initially Tara's mother was reluctant to send her daughter to Star again but Binodini's cajoling did the trick. When nine-year-old Tara went to Star with Aghorenath Pathak her self-confidence amazed everyone. She received training in acting from Amritalal Mitra and Amritalal Bose, in singing from Ramratan Sanyal and in dancing from Kashinath Chattopadhyay, She acted as a Bhil boy in *Nasiram* on 25 May 1888, and then as Gopal in Sarala on 22 September 1888. She achieved fame in a number of roles as young boys. Tara finally got the opportunity to act in a female role in 1889 as Hemangini in Girish Ghosh's *Haranidhi.* Thus began her journey. Under Girish's direction, Tara acted as Mukulji in *Chanda* and as Britannia in *Palashir Judhha* of Nabin Chandra Sen. When the leading lady of Star, Prova left for Minerva, Tara played the roles of Bibi in *Tajjab Byapar*, and Tarubala in *Tarubala.* At the age of thirteen, Tara performed the difficult roles of Chaitanya in *Chaitanya Leela*, Damayanti in *Naladamayanti* and Gopa in *Buddhadev* creditably. She also performed roles where she had to sing (which was her toughest task). These included Bangabhasha, Dhruva and Radhika. She then performed as Bijoy in *Bijoybasanta*, Gauri in

Annadamangal, Rebecca in *Bahut Achha*, Mahila in *Babu*, Bilashini in *Bibaha Bibhrat*, and then Saibalini in *Chandrasekhar*.

She had left the theatre at the age of fifteen when she was offered financial security by a lover after only three nights of performing as Saibalini. Then Girish Chandra called her to join Minerva for the role of Karameti Bai in the play of the same name. Unable to refuse him, she agreed to perform for a few nights. Then after a long gap she joined forces with Amarendranath when he formed the Indian Dramatics Club. She performed in the plays of *Palashir Juddha* and *Bellick Bazar* in Emerald Theatre. Then she repeated her performance when the plays were performed later at Minerva. Soon afterwards when City Theatre performed at Emerald she acted there for a few nights as Devi in *Devi Chowdhurani*. Her performance was hailed as the better one than being performed in Bengal theatre. Soon afterwards, when Classic was established by Amarendranath, Tara joined him despite the court case that had disrupted their relationship earlier. After leaving Classic, Tara stayed away from all theatres for some time and later joined Star. There she performed the roles of Aparna in *Kironshashi* and a small role in Dwijendralal Roy's *Biraha*. That performance in the cameo role of a neighbour won for her the role of Saibya in *Harishchandra* and then the lead roles in *Basantasena* and *Adarshabandhu*. In 1897, she performed the role of Annapurna in Girish Ghosh's play *Mayabasaan* and soon afterwards gave in to Amarendranath's cajoling to joining Classic. There she performed as Kaikeyi in *Ram Banabashe* and then the lead role of Golendam in *Moner Moton* in 1901. Around this time, Tarasundari was offered a large bonus and inducted in the newly-established Arora Theatre. There she performed as Mokshada in *Kal Porinoy* for which she received a gold medal from zamindar Anath Nath Dev.

According to many, the role of Riziya was Tarasundari's greatest claim to fame. According to Aparesh Mukhopadhay, Tarasundari's lifelong companion from around this time and the father of her two children, the revolutionary Bipin Chandra Pal considered Tarasundari's performance of Riziya as far better than any European or American production. Another famous role she performed at this theatre, which changed its name to Unique, was Mondamala in *Ratnamala*. She only worked here for a few months and then joined Minerva. There she acted as Bama in *Samsar*, Kalyani in *Pratapaditya*, Joshibai in *Rana Pratap*, Gauri in *Haragauri*, Saraswati in *Balidaan*, Johra in *Sirajuddaula*, etc., and helped make Minerva the leading theatre in Calcutta at that time. Then another new theatre, Kohinoor, came up and Sarat Kumar Roy spent enormous amounts of money to procure the best actors and actresses from the different theatres of the city. Tarasundari was lured to Kohinoor and performed in *Chandbibi* as the main role. In *Shivaji* she was Lakshmibai but within a year the theatre shut down. Tara joined a new theatre called Bani and performed in the plays that were already running. She then rejoined Minerva and performed as Padmavati in *Ashoka*, Sunetra in *Tapobal*, Kashmiri Begum in *Durgadas*, Jahanara in *Shahjahan*, Nurjahan in *Nurjahan*, and Biraja in *Grihalakshmi* admirably. Then she acted as Kuveni in the new play *Singhal Bijoy* by Dwijendralal Roy to a packed auditorium. Thereafter, she performed as Doranalini in Aparesh Chandra Mukhopadhyay's *Shubhadrishti* and as Mokshada in Amritalal Bose's *Khashdakhal*. Tara then rejoined Star and took part in two new productions: Utpal in Kshirode Prasad Bidyabinode's opera *Kinnari* and a main role in Aparesh's opera *Urvashi*. After her last performance of Riziya in 1933 at the age of 55, Tarasundari quit the stage and went in to retirement at Bhuvaneshwar. She passed away on 19 April 1948.

Tarasundari had another side to her talented personality and that is evident in the poems published in two editions of Girish Ghosh's journal *Saurabh* (1895–Sravan and Bhadra). They were *Prabaher Rupantar* and *Kusum O Bramar*.

Tinkadi Dasi (1870–1926): Performance (1887–1917)

Tinkadi was one of the brightest stars in the early years of theatre. She was brought up by her mother who earned her living as a prostitute but was miserly. Despite the fact that Tinkadi had a melodious voice, her mother would not spend the money required for her training. Her plan was that as soon as Tinkadi came of age she would sell her to a rich patron who would be able to keep her as a mistress. But she had not reckoned with Tinkadi's love for the arts. From the moment she went to watch *Meghnad Badh* of Girish Ghosh, Tinkadi could only dream of joining the theatre. But it was difficult for a newcomer to join the theatre where stalwarts like Sukumari, Binodini and others held sway. Finally in 1887, she got a chance to perform in Girish Ghosh's *Bilwamangal* though she had no speaking part. Luckily Tinkadi performed in a song when one of the girls fell ill. Her performance was outstanding that day and the one rupee she was given to have sweets, she treasured till the end of her days. As Star Theatre was being rebuilt, the company went to Dhaka to perform. Tinkadi, however, was not allowed to follow the company. She then joined a private theatrical company for some time. When Bina Theatre was started by Rajkrishna Roy, Tinkadi joined it on a salary of Rs. 20 a month. But it was a short-lived venture. Then she was co-opted in to Gopal Lal Sil's Emerald Theatre at double the salary. Soon this theatre too closed down. In the meantime, Tinkadi's mother was trying to fix her up with a rich patron. They were willing to pay her a maintenance and compensate her mother on the condition she left the theatre. Tinkadi refused to give up acting. No amount of cajoling or punishment could move her and finally her mother had to give up. Tinkadi joined City Theatre where she performed in *Sarala*, *Bilwalmangal*, *Chaitanya Leela*, *Tarubala*, and *Shadhabar Ekadashi*.

While in City Theatre Tinkadi went to perform in Kali Krishna Tagore's house during the Puja festivities. Also present there as a guest, Girish Ghosh was witness to her performance. After the show, he praised her acting and said that she would be one of the greatest actresses of Bengal one day. Sometime later Girish sent for her when he was appointed manager and playwright of Minerva. She was given a contract for a year at a salary of Rs. 30 a month. Initially, she did not have a role in any play and Pramadasundaari was asked to play Lady Macbeth in a production. Soon enough, Girish replaced the latter with Tinkadi. In 1905, she also acted as Bimala in the adapted version of Bankim's *Durgeshnandini* in Minerva as well as Sree in *Sitaram*—performances which she was remembered for. There was much gossip around Tinkadi and Girish Ghosh, that their relationship was much more than that of a teacher–student. It is undoubtedly true that she consulted Girish in all the important decisions she took not only in her professional career but in her personal life as well even though she was loyal to the babu/protector with whom she lived. She worked with Girish until she quit acting when she fell ill in 1917. She was diabetic which meant that she could not keep late hours. On Ghosh's advice, she worked with a private theatre, the Thespian Theatre. But soon ill health forced her to give up acting and she died in 1926. Her will stated that two houses she owned were to be given to Mayo Hospital in Burrabazar and a third to the son of her babu. All her jewels and furniture were to be sold and Rs. 50 each to be given to her tenants and the rest spent in her funeral rites.

KIRONBALA (1868–90): PERFORMANCE (1887–90)

Kironbala made a name for herself in theatre in a very short time though she came from a backward and uneducated family. She joined the theatre at the age of thirteen and died at the age of twenty-two. Her success was undoubtedly due to good fortune because she was trained to be an understudy of Binodini in secret by Girish Ghosh who feared that Binodini might leave the theatre at the pinnacle of her glory. There was considerable apprehension among the critics as to whether Kiron would be able to emulate the high standard of acting that Binodini had set. Kiron, however, justified the faith that her mentor reposed in her. She performed the role of Rangini of *Bellick Bazar* with élan and then in 1887 acted in *Rup O Sanatan*. Her greatest role was as Sarala in *Swarnalata* in 1888 in the new theatre of Star. She also excelled in the role of Gyanada in *Prafulla* and as Kamala in *Haranidhi*, which was her last role. She contracted small pox and died in 1890.

NAGENDRABALA: PERFORMANCE (1889–1932)

Nagendrabala excelled in performing character roles. She had the ability to change her voice according to the character she had to enact no matter the age of the character. Instructed by Girish Ghosh, in her long career she performed with a number of great actors and actresses. She was easily able to adapt to the various styles of acting that were popular at various times, and was at her best in performing in light, comic roles. She worked at different times in Star, Royal Bengal and Minerva Theatres. She started her career as Sushila in Girish's *Haranidhi*. Then she performed as Gunjamaka in *Chanda*, as Tarala in *Molina Bikash*, as Shanta in *Tarubala*, as Lakshmi in *Mahapuja* and as Bindu in *Mayabshan*. After nine years in Star, she joined Royal Bengal Theatre but did not get any good role. The theatre itself was on the verge of collapse and with the death of its leader Biharilal Chattopadhyay, it folded up. Nagendrabala then joined Minerva Theatre and till the end of her life remained attached to it.

In 1905, she acted in Girish's *Balidaan* as Rajlakshmi and later as Saraswati. She then performed as Shireen in *Shiree Farhad*, as Ramabai in *Dalita Phoni* and as Mrinalini in *Mrinalini*. She was so closely attached with Minerva she never left though there were many changes in management. Between 1905 and 1922, in many plays, she had to remain as understudy or was chosen in very small roles but she never abandoned Minerva. She never even left when Minerva had no stage of its own and on Alfred stage she acted as Rebati in *Jiban Judhha*. In the new premises in 1925, she acted as Nibritti in *Atmadarshan*. In the next two plays *Bangali* and *Byapika Biday*, Nagendrabala achieved resounding success. In 1928, her acting as Tripurasundari in *Jatichyuta*, was considered to be 'acting without being acting' by *Nachghar*. Her last role was as Jora in *Debjani* in 1932.

Kusumkumari (1876–1948): Performance (1892–1933)

Born in 1876, Kusumkumari won fame in Minerva. Unlike the other actresses, she came to Minerva not as a child but as a young girl of seventeen in 1892. Proficient in singing and dancing, Kusum did not have to climb up to leading roles from the bottom. She never had to work in the chorus but was given an important role in *Macbeth* in the 1893 production. Up to 1896, Kusum was associated with Minerva and performed in plays like *Mukul Manjari*, *Abu Hossain*, *Swapner Phool*, *Karametibai*, *Prafulla*, *Phonir Moni*, etc. In 1897, Kusum known as the 'Jewel of Minerva Theatre' joined Amarendranath Dutta's Classic and performed as Marjina in *Alibaba*. She was not only successful in singing and dancing but proved to be a great actress. She gained fame as the first woman trainer in dancing. She was Amarendranath's mistress after his break-up with Tarasundari and performed with him in Gramaphone recordings. She performed as Bhramar in an adaptation of *Krishnakanter Will* of the same name and won praise in the leading newspaper *Indian Mirror* in 1899. The newspaper said that the transition from a 'playful kitten to a responsible wife' was a difficult one for stage presentation. 'The earlier portion of her life is one of loving, ingenuousness and not of archness such as is exhibited by the interpreter. The transition into graver mood however is in the care of the player, an artistic achievement.' Though she had no formal education she performed in English in *Macbeth* and *Richard III* as Lady Macbeth and Lady Anne. She ended her acting career in Natyaniketan. Under the aegis of Art Theatre, she performed Sachidebi with great finesse in *Sri Gauranga* at Star Theatre under the direction of Aparesh Chandra. She retired from her career in 1933 and finally died in seclusion in 1948.

SUSHILABALA/SUSHILASUNDARI (1884–1915): PERFORMANCE (1892–1914)

Sushilabala came to be known as Prima Donna Nightingale at the height of her acting career. She was born in 1884 and at the age of ten passed Middle Bengali examinations from Jhamapukur A.M. Girls' School but could not continue her studies due to financial problems. She had a beautiful singing voice and in 1893 when Minerva was established by Nagendrabhusan Mukhopdhayay, Sushilabala entered as a trainee. After some time, Gaiety theatrical group was established in Bina Theatre where she joined without any remuneration. Her performance as Hemangini in Girish Ghosh's *Haranidhi* was so superlative that she was immediately contracted on a fixed salary. But the group vanished soon. She then joined a private theatre called Empress Theatre where Ardhendusekhar was the dramatic director. She also came into contact with the great actress of the time Tinkadi Dasi and Girish Ghosh and travelled with them for some time. In the meantime, the zamindar of Sripur Narendra Nath Sarkar wanted to restart Minerva though he was very young. He was also very attracted to Sushilabala's singing talent and brought her as the leading actress to Minerva. She performed in *Sree*, *Madalasa*, and, *Madhabi Kankan*. Narendranath then weaned away Girish from Classic as Director. Sushilabala performed as Jayati in *Sitaram* and excelled in her singing and acting. She was then living with Narendranath who on gaining maturity had become the manager of Minerva. But despite the popularity of the plays Minerva could not be financially successful and soon Narendranath had to declare himself insolvent. Sushilabala quit and joined Minerva. Her salary was fixed at Rs. 80 initially but her brilliant performance forced them to increase it to Rs. 100. She excelled in performance in Minerva in the play *Balidan*. When conflicts arose between Star management and Dwijendralal Roy over the inclusion of Girish Ghosh's popular poem 'Haldighater Yuddha' in *Rana Pratap*, Roy dissociated himself from Star and took the play to Minerva. Sushilabala acted as Meher. She was very popular in Dwijendralal Roy's plays where her songs drew large audiences. Around this time in 1906, National Theatre authorities tried to force her into a contract with a bonus of Rs. 1,000—and a monthly salary of Rs. 120. When Monomohon Pandey got wind of this proposal he was annoyed and worried. They tore up her contract and made Sushilabala sign a three-year contract with Minerva authorities with a bonus of Rs. 1,000—and a monthly salary of Rs. 110. Unfortunately the Minerva authorities could never forgive Sushilabala for her inclination towards National Theatre and soon after the contract was signed they refused to give her lead roles. Sushila did not like this ill treatment and wrote a letter in 1907 to Monomohon Pandey informing the authorities that she was willing to return the bonus if they would release her from the contract. The authorities were furious and since an advertisement had already been released that Sushilabala would act as Meherunnissa in *Rana Pratap* they were set to lose a lot of money. There were also rumours that Sushila was being wooed by Kohinoor Theatre as well. A legal confrontation took place and ended in Sushilabala's defeat. It was only after a period that she could leave Minerva.

Sushilabala then joined Amarendranath in 1911 and all the while supported the ailing Narendra Nath. She performed in many roles under Amarendra Nath's direction in Star and left the stage in 1914 when she was pregnant. But the baby was stillborn and though she rejoined the stage, her health was irrevocably damaged. She succumbed to her illness in 1915.

NARISUNDARI (1877–1939):
PERFORMANCE (1892–1926)

The famous singer-actress Narisundari was born in 1877 and joined the theatre in 1892. It is not known whether she trained in her youth but she amazed the public with her classical music performances on stage. Many of the theatre songs which she popularized were later recorded for posterity by the Gramaphone Record Company. But she also gained popularity in roles of simple women. In 1892, she appeared first in Star as Rishyasringa and then as Dalani Begum in *Chandrasekhar* in 1894. In 1901, she excelled as Suryamukhi in *Bishabriksha* in Star. Narisundari worked for nineteen years in Star and despite many ups and downs in the fortunes of the theatre did not abandon it though many attempts were made to lure her away by rival theatres. She acted in different roles in 41 plays in Star. Finally in 1911 she joined Minerva with a bonus of Rs 5,000. She performed as Chaya in *Chandragupta* and then as Bedamata in *Tapobal*. She then rejoined Star where she stayed from 1912 to 1914. She acted as Aparajita in Amarendra Nath Dutta's *Abhinetrir Rup*. In 1915, she again joined Minerva as Leela in Dwijendralal Roy's *Singhal Bijay*. After 1916, she left regular acting but occasionally performed in some specific roles of her choice like Susangeeti in *Swapna Basabadatta* in Star in 1921. Her last performance was in Mitra Theatre on Alfred Stage in *Sri Durga*. She then adopted a religious life and died in seclusion in 1939.

NIRODASUNDARI (1889–1973): PERFORMANCE (1898–)

Nirodasundari's career spanned the whole period under discussion in this book, starting with Girish Ghosh and ending with Sisir Bhaduri. She was born in 1889 in a slum near present Girish Park and her mother Tarangini was acquainted with Kusumkumari. She joined theatre at the age of nine. It was Kusumkumari who brought her to Amarendranath Dutta and who adopted her and taught her to sing, dance, and act. She danced in the chorus in *Dol Leela* in Classic in 1989. At the end of the year she got the role of Bansari in *Nirmala*. In 1901, Amarendra Nath decided that Nirodasundari was old enough to have an important role and cast her as Adhira in his play *Guptakatha*. But when Classic Theatre closed Nirodasundari was only seventeen. She had to join a travelling theatre which paid her a paltry sum of rupees four daily. Finally in 1911, this life of uncertainly ended when Minerva took her in.. Girish Ghosh was the manager there and though he was plagued by ill health, Nirodasundari was a student of his inspired guidance. In 1911, she acted as Deepi in a farce *Jhakmari* and then acted in *Rakampher* followed by Dwijendralal's *Chandragupta* and Girish's *Tapobal*. She excelled in Girish's *Grihalakshmi* in 1912 and in Kshirodeprasad's *Aheriya*. For a short time, she joined Monomohan Theatre and then returned to Minerva. She performed Chambada's role very well in Aparesh Chandra's *Ramanuja*. After the performance she was blessed by Sri Ramkrishna's consort Sarada Devi. In 1918, her performances in *Kinnori* also became very popular. In Madan Theatre she joined Sisir Kumar's group in *Alamgir*. When Sisir Kumar left Madan and formed Natyamandir he could rely on Nirodasundari's support. She acted as Tungabhadra in *Seeta*. She also acted as Satyabati in Dwijendralal Roy's *Bhishma*. Towards the end of her life she joined Minerva.

CHARUSHILA: PERFORMANCE (1908–35)

Charushila first came in to public notice in 1908 as Meenabibi in the opera *Tufani* in Minerva. It is not known when exactly she joined

Minerva. Between 1908 and 1921, she earned fame as the 'ballet girl' and acted in operas and farces like *Jhakmari*. She was able to bag a role as Saudamini in Dwijendralal's *Punarjanma* and this success again brought her the role of Rambha in Girish Ghosh's *Tapobal*. In 1912, she was given the role of Amina in *Dariya* and Kumudini in *Grihalakshmi*. Between 1914 and 1921, she acted in a number of plays in Minerva. Shortly after, Minerva Theatre caught fire and Charushila was advised to join another theatre. She, however, did not want to abandon Minerva in its time of need. In 1924 when Minerva hired the Alfred Stage she performed as Madhuri in *Jibanjudhha*. She was always grateful to Ardhendusekhar for bringing in acting roles in the midst of her dancing career in Minerva.

In 1925, Charushila joined Sisir Kumar Ghosh's Natyamandir and performed as Rani Gunabati in Rabindranath Tagore's *Bisharjan*. From 1925 to 1929, she acted in numerous popular roles in Natyamandir—Draupadi in *Nara Narayan* (1926), as the title role in Sarat Chandra's *Shoroshi* (1927), as Dai in *Abu Hossain*, as Natabar in *Hashnuhana* and, as Siraji Begum in *Digbijoyee* (1928). The final play at Natyamandir was *Harano Ratan* where she acted as Jhanjhamoyee. Then when Sisir Kumar left for America, Charu joined Minerva. She acted as Sulochana in *Abhijata* in 1931, Nayaleela in *Basuki* and Rani Sandhya in *Purohitin* 1932. Her last role was as Bidya in *Bidyasundar*.

Niharbala (1898–1954): Performance (1918/1921—around 1931)

Niharbala joined Star Theatre where she was associated for a long time from the age of twenty-three. She acted as Zeenat in Aparesh Chandra's *Ayodhyar Begum* in 1921. She was a great performer and dancer and her ability to pick up dances simply by watching them has been testified to by Ahindra Chowdhury. Her style of dancing was very different from that followed in the early years of Bengali theatre. Her performance in *Phullara* in 1929 in Star was highly praised in *Nachghar* and her dance movements of arms, body and feet were said to be full of grace. Despite the fact that Star had more famous actresses like Tarasundari, Niharbala's sensuous dancing fascinated the audience. Aparesh gave Niharbala an opportunity to showcase her talent in almost all the plays being performed. Niharbala also choreographed the dances and trained other girls. In 1923, Art Theatre took up the task of managing Star Theatre and in 1923 Aparesh Chandra's *Karnarjun* was performed. It was a great hit in acting, production, and music and was praised in all the newspapers. Niharbala acted as Niyati in it and her singing and dancing gained much popularity. In 1924 in Aparesh Chandra's *Iraner Rani*, Niharbala performed a new type of dance which also captured the audience's imagination. The next test for Niharbala was performing in Rabindranath Tagore's *Chirakumar Sabha*. The music director was Dinendranath Tagore and doubts arose if the actresses of the public theatre would be able to capture the delicate nuances of Rabindranath's plays. But with Dinendranath's guidance and her dedication Niharbala mesmerized the poet himself with her singing and performance.

In 1931, she joined the newly-established Natya Niketan under Probodh Chandra Guha. She acted in many plays here but gradually became more interested in the spiritual life in Pondicherry Ashram. She became a disciple of Sri Aurobindo and the public theatre lamented the loss of a great actress and dancer. She died in 1954.

Prova Debi (1903–52): Performance (1921–52)

Prova Debi joined theatre at the age of eighteen as a ballet girl under Sisir Kumar Bhaduri's direction in the Bengal Theatrical Company established by the Madans. She was an amazing singer and her quality of voice was unique. She performed as Rupkumari in *Alamgir* in 1921 but due to managerial differences with the Madans, Sisir Kumar left. The Madans brought in Nirmalendu Lahiri and in 1922 Prova acted as Sarama in *Ratneshwar Mandir*. With Sisir Bhaduri Prora became one of the star performers in 1930s and 1940s. Prova wrote number of songs published in *Nachghar*.

Krishnabhamini (1893?–1933): Performance (1921–32)

Krishnabhamini was brought to Star by Aparesh Chandra Mukhopadhyay in 1921 for the new play *Mandakini*, but Krishnabhamini could not leave a mark. In the next play she performed as Chhaya in *Ayodhyar Begum* and this time it got her a mention in the newspapers, with critics claiming that it was indeed original acting. This play began the trend of the matinee show on Sunday in Star Theatre. In 1922, Krishnabhamini performed Chinmoy in *Nawabi*, Urvashi in *Apsara* and

Krishna in *Sudama.* Her competitors in the plays were the leading lady Tarasundari and Niharbala but even as a new actress Krishnabhamini was able to please her mentor Aparesh Chandra. Soon Aparesh despite Tarasundari's displeasure handed over the responsibility of Star to Art Theatre and in 1923, in the new play *Karnarjun* was able to establish herself as an actress in the role of Padmini. In August of the same year, in Rabindranath's *Raja O Rani,* Krishnabhamini played the role of Queen Sumitra. In Dwijendralal Roy's *Chandragupta,* she was Chhaya where her singing was more inspired than her acting. In 1924, she took the lead role in *Iraner Rani.* In 1924, on the occasion of Good Friday was launched *Muktir Dak* which was the first One Act in Bengali and Krishnabhamini was its leading lady as Amba. In *Bibaha Bibhrat* she was the maid. A story circulates that initially she was offended at getting that role but when she heard that Kshetramoni got a reference in Lady Dufferin's autobiography she was inspired to give a great performance.

Another important event in her life was during the performance of the play *Sarala* in 1925 in the title role when she realized that the elderly Binodini was in the auditorium watching the play. When it was over Binodini came over and praised her for a fine performance—a great honour for Krishnabhamini. She performed as Arzmad in *Golcunda* (1925) and as Kironmoyee in *Balidan.* Around this time Star was facing internal problems and Krishnabhamini left Star in 1926 and joined Sisir Bhaduri's Natyamandir. In his new style of training Krishnabhamini excelled as Padma in *Naranarayan,* Kamalmoni in Rabindranath's *Shesh Raksha* (1927), Hashnuhana in the play with the same name (1928) Sitara in *Digvijay.* Soon the competition with Prova and Kankaboti became too overpowering and Krishnabhamini left Natyamandir to return to Star under Art Theatre. In 1929, in *Chaitanya Leela,* she took up Binodini's mantle in performing the role of Nimai. In *Mantra Shakti* (1929) she was Bani, in *Swayambara* (1931) she was Savitri, in *Sri Gaurango* she was Bishnupriya and in *Poshyaputra* (1932) she was Shivani where she is said to have scored another triumph. That was also her last role.

Kankaboti Sahoo (1903–39): Performance (1929–39)

The entrance of Kankaboti Sahoo to the world of theatre was as dramatic as any play she ever performed in. She was born in Muzaffarpur to an actress mother and a zamindar and honorary Magistrate father, Gadadhar Sahoo. He was a man of extraordinary liberal temperament and his own love for instrumental music led him to organize musical soirees in his house and train his two daughters, Kankaboti and Chandraboti in music along with academics. He sent his daughters to Calcutta to pursue further studies but was liberal enough to be supportive when one daughter Chandraboti joined films and the other Kanakaboti joined theatre.

Kanakaboti graduated from Bethune College where she realized her potential in fine arts and decided not to continue with the post graduation she had started. She signed a three-year contract with Art Theatre that she would undergo compulsory training for some months and only then would she be eligible to perform in a play and earn a salary. She also had to attend a training camp for three months. Soon posters were put up around the town that a new graduate actress Kankaboti would be performing in a new play. During this time she came into contact with Sisir Bhaduri and was impressed by his training. Sisir started a poster war with Art Theatre saying that Kankaboti Sahoo, B.A. had joined Natyamandir. Soon Kankaboti had to face a lawsuit from Probodh Chandra Guha of Art Theatre. A veritable drama occurred in court when Sisir Bhaduri appeared along with Kankaboti and the case after many twists and turns was settled out of court. But Kankaboti was instructed to complete some more months at Art Theatre before she could join Sisir Bhaduri. At this time many of the theatre critics were unhappy at the thought of the actress playing one theatre against another and reaping undeserving benefits as well as support from an actor who was so respected in society for having singlehandedly made acting a respectable profession.

Everyone waited with baited breath as to which play and in which theatre would she make her debut. Finally, Sisir Kumar too realized that it was necessary strategy to bring her into the limelight as soon as possible, in order to seal their victory in the case. . They waited till her term at Art Theatre ended and then she could legally make her appearance. There were many unkind statements being made in the newspapers of the time questioning whether it was worth for two established prestigious theatres to fight over an actress who was yet to prove her substance. Speculation about her qualities and capabilities was rife since it was rumoured that not only had she performed in drama and singing in Bethune College but that she was so good in singing

Rabindra Sangeet that her performance of the song '*ei lobhinu shongo tobo shundor he shundor*' in Jorashanko had greatly pleased and moved Rabindranath himself. Finally, in February 1929, Kankaboti emerged from the shadows to perform as Bharatnaari in *Digvijay*, directed by Sisir Kumar. Finally, all speculations were laid to rest. Sisir Bhaduri, in order to put her musical talent to use, created the play *Basanta Leela* in which Kankaboti charmed everyone in the role of Sri Krishna. In the meantime Sisir Kumar married Kankaboti and continued his experimentation with her. In *Bisharjan* too Kanka had a male role as Jaysingha. But though her singing was commended, her acting was not. In between two plays in June 1929, Sisir Kumar organized a music programme by Kankaboti. That claimed the unstinting praise of critics but her acting in the plays despite the training of Sisir Kumar was considered unsatisfactory, especially in comparison to Krishnabhamini. However, her performance as Buddha's mother Gautami in *Buddhhadev Charita* was deemed to be immaculate. Yet, critics considered her performance as Jathaima (aunt) in *Roma* to be inadequate in comparison to Tarasundari's portrayal in Art Theatre. Sisir Kumar then decided to experiment with Rabindranath's *Tapati* which the poet had recently performed in Jorasanko. Here Kankaboti had the role of Bipasha. Despite Sisir's efforts, the audience did not like the play and Natyamandir suffered financially. But all agreed that Kankaboti's rendition of three Rabindra Sangeets were extraordinary. In 1930, Natyamandir's lease was not renewed by Madan Company and in this period of distress Natyamandir was faced with the lawsuit by Charushila for non-payment of dues. So, Charushilas's roles had to be managed by Kankaboti. She kept trying to cope with the situation by changing roles in the old plays.

Soon Star requested Sisir Bhaduri to perform under the Art Theatre banner when Ahindra Chowdhury left Art Theatre to join Minerva. Sisir started with *Chirakumar Sabha*, which had been so successful at Natyamandir. Kankaboti who had joined him was Nirbala but though her songs were appreciated critics claimed that her large body, which was unsuitable for the character, had distracted the audience from her acting. In reality, Kankaboti was no match for Niharbala's rendition of Nirbala. Soon Kankaboti joined Sisir Kumar and leading actress Prova Devi when he decided to take his troupe on a visit to America for a performance at Broadway. The trip was not without its disappointments and humiliations and finally they returned in 1931 and soon joined Rangmahal who offered a stage at Cornwallis Street. In *Sri Sri Bishnupriya* Kankaboti was Sachimata, though praised for her performance generated controversy because Sisir Bhaduri was criticized for partiality towards her. Criticism continued with Jijabai's role in *Gairik Pataka* more so because her mistakes in pronunciation were not forgiven since she was highly educated. After the connection with Rangmahal ended, Kankaboti in Natyaniketan, performed in two roles: Gandhari and Rukmini in *Mahaprasthan* in 1932. Kankaboti left Natyaniketan in 1933 following her husband's footsteps and a new lease at Star saw a new play *Abhimanini* where Kanka performed the character Bala very well.

In February 1932, the first play for children, *Phuler Aayna* was launched with Kanka 's help. This was followed by *Biraj Bou* under the newly-named Naba Natyamandir in which Kankaboti was Biraj and her performance was admired by all. In *Sarama* in 1934, Kankaboti was Mandodari where her dignified performance was again received very well. In November 1934, *Dosher Daabi* was launched where Kankaboti was Sujata in which she performed and sang well. In December 1934 when *Bijaya* based on Sarat Chandra Chattopadhyay's story 'Dotta' was launched, Rabindranath who was an admirer of Sisir Bhaduri's performance, promised to write a play for him. Finally, Jogajog was handed over to Sisir and on 25 December 1926, *Jogajog* was performed with Kankaboti as Kumudini. Many had reservations regarding the casting of Kankaboti as Kumudini since the description of Kumudini was that of a slim and tall girl and Kankaboti did not match up to the description at all. But as Kanka's sister, Chandrabati who was present at the play, described later, Rabindranath hugged Kankaboti after watching the play and told her that her performance had made him forget the disparity of her appearance. In 1939, during the performance of Mura in *Chandragupta* of Dwijendralal, Kankaboti fell ill on stage and was diagnosed with meningitis. Despite all efforts of the doctors at Carmichael Medical College, Kankaboti passed away in 1939. Along with her acting career, Kankaboti remained till the end a faithful wife always supporting her eccentric and artistic husband in all his ventures and left a son and a daughter behind.

APPENDICES

TARASUNDARI

PROBAHER RUPANTAR

Smashan Jibonshomo, Nandan Kananshomo,
Paapsmriti dure gechhe, phutechhe nayan.
Jiboner gurubhar, kator na kore aar,
Ke Amar? Ghuchailo bhrama achhadan.
Kshudramoti naaripran, artha, asha, abhimaan
Kaaler kuteel srote hoye dishahara
Andhakaar aalingan, koriachhi aajibon
Prolobhane shonpi mon hoiaachhi shara.
Saral Asroy kore, praner aaabegbhore
Dhorite giyachhi jaare, she noy amar.
Hashimukhe theli paye, andha mon tare chay
Porinaame othe shudhu sreanto hahakar.
Sohodor, shohodora, praner shongini jara,
Swarther chholone bhuli, kore atmaboli.
Bhalobashi Jodi kare, nana kotha koy tare,
Katore hridoy bhare, dibanishi jwoli
E kotha bujhibe ke re? duhitay chhuri mere
Mata kore anweshan sukha aponaar.
Chhai e hridoypur, jak bhenge hok chur,
Aakinchan swarthasidhhi mulmantra tar.
Poromayu joto kshoy, sukha aasha toto hoy
Bardhokyer shone bare, laalosha jibone.
Porokaal chinta hay, oshar swapan pray,
Chute jay ekebare, chhaya nai mone.
Bhabishyat bibhishika, pretmoyee morichika,
Protikriti Jodi tar, milechhe aamar.
Joubon probritti joto, shourobhe koribe roto,
Porimol pobitrata koro anushar.

Change of Flow

My life that reeked of death is now a paradise
Gone are the shadows of sin from my eyes;
The sad weight of time hurts me no more!
Who ripped the veil of ignorance?
A woman blind of vision have I chased
Wealth hope and vision
Confounded by the darkness of the times
Have I embraced phantoms all my life
Succumbing to temptations and death
An innocent soul, have I desired what was not mine
My blind passion embraces Love that scorns,
All comes to nought in grief and tears.
The dear ones are tempted by avarice to sacrifice me
They scorn my love and fill my days with torment
Who knows the mystery of a mother,
who seeks pleasure in a daughter's death?
O my heart, turn to ashes, be crushed
By desire and avarice at the roots!
Alas! As my days come to their end I thirst for happiness!
Old age whets desire and life beyond is but a mirage,
That races around without shade.
Future is nightmare
A ghostly horror am I!
Make fragrant your youthful passion
Seek purity while your sun shines!

(Translated by Dr Purna Chowdhury)[1]

Kusum O Bhramar

i

Milay kamal kay, prokritir kolay,
Chhanite madhuri hori, dhoray ki bhab dhori
Aanilo chumiya kul, mridu mridu dole,
Kantay bhorechhe gaye, tobu mon bhole?

ii

Prem aashe aashe jay, premik bhramar?
Onador naahi kore, shomador jaare tare,
Modhu khaye, shukhe boshe-buker opor.
Bojha day, ke tome aaponar por.

iii

Naarir jobon shomo, gorob tomar,
Jotodin modhu robe, aadorer dhon hobe,
Abohele bilaile, maan aaponar.
Na bukhile chholona e kutil dhorar.

iv

Subash dhorechho buke, ki hetu chhorao?
Guner gorima naai, ojotone bujhi tai
Sadher shorabh hay! Obadhe lutao.
Bikriti prokriti loye kiba such pao?

v

Bichitra choritre mugdha, antar aamar
Kheliye paban mone, sumodhur aabahone,
Porag chhoraye more de'ko na'ko aar-
Anumatro pore aachhi dhore e shonshaar.

The Flower and the Bee

i

The rose languishes in nature's lap
Essence of earthly beauty
Swaying to the wind
Lures, despite thorns.

ii

Love is transient, the lover a bee!
It showers love and sucks the nectar
Perched on breasts
The lover and the stranger are one.

iii

Your vanity, woman, is fleeting
Like your youth
Cherished when succulent,
Thou shall be thy passion's slave
You give away your honour;
O Innocence, you never fathomed
The ways of this wicked world.

iv

Why are your breasts fragrant?
Blind to your own virtues
You give yourself away too easily;
How does corrupt nature make you happy?

v

I am baffled by human nature!
Donot beckon me
with sweet words and fragrant voices;
I cling to the corner of life.

(Translation by Dr Purna Chowdhury)

BINODINI DASI

(from her collection of poems called *Basana*)

SMRITI

Smriti lo bisher jwala diyo nako aar,
E shonghsare chirodin kichhui na roy;
Tobe keno dukho tumi dao onibar
Tumi mone hole prane jwala otishoy.
Osthay shongshar kichhu chirosthayi noy,
Sukha dukkha chirodin ghore shomobhabe;
Kaaler kobole shobe hoye jaabe loy.
Ananta nidrar kolay ghumabe nishchinte.
Kale nara bhule shob kaalete baleen,
Chirodin nahi kichhu rohe sukha aar.
Tothapi shokole rohe tomar adhin;
Shokoli bhulite pare tore bhola bhar.
Ja hobar hoiachhe purechhe hridoy,
Kebol bisher jwala smarane tomar.
Ekhon jibon momo smashan aaloy.
Tobuo tomar chinta dohe anibar.
Doya ko're bhul more shoktiswarupini,
Smriti hote bismritite adhik shantosh.
Chhariye aashsar aasha hoyechhi dukkhini;
Aapona bhulile pore aaro poritosh.

Memory

Memory dear, torment me with your poison no more.
Nothing endures in this universe of ours
Why then do you pain and distress me so?
Your presence brings agonizing hours.
Nothing is permanent in this transient world
Joy and sorrow make their turns on the wheel
Time will finally destroy it all
And in the lap of eternal rest will we sleep.
In time Man forgets, into Time Man goes.
No worldly joy will last.
Oblivion permits all but oblivion of you
You have us all in your grasp.
It has happened as it would, my heart has been seared
The ache and memory are all that remain.
My life is a now an abode of . . .

Yet your memory brings agony and pain.
Shaktiswarupini, forget me, oh let me be.
There's comfort in oblivion, not in recall-
I've crossed Hope's boundaries and brought myself grief,
There's solace in forgetting self, forgetting all.

(Translated by Dr Sipra Mukherjee)[2]

Ekti Golaap

Kar tore phutechho lo golaap shundori
  Ke tore aador kore
  Ke rakhe hridoy pore
Kar jonye chharatechho ruper madhuri.
Bolo kar aadorete tumi aadorini
  Ke tomay bhalobashe
  Kar sukha-shadh aashe
Porechho sundor shaj olo shohagini.
Ki ba kotha bol tor shomirono shone
  Dule dule dhole dhole
  Heshe heshe gole gole
Adore shohage bhore anandita mone.
Janona ki chirokaal thake na aador
  Aji prophullito mone
  Mishye shohago shone
Jar kotha kohitechho ananda antar.
Dui din pore tumi dekhio aabar.
  Tomar she prandhon
  Anonde bibhor mon
Onyo phule kore paan mmodhu anibar.
Ekhon aadore tore hridoye dhorechhe
  Kale naahi robe ghor
  Bhangibe swapan tor
Dekhibi anyer preme shohage mojechhe.
Tyaji tor bhalobasha bhulechhe shokol
  Kandile na phire chabe
  Shadhile na kotha kobe
Kamal hridoye shaar hobe asrujol.

A Rose

For whom hast thou blossomed, O beautiful Rose?
Who will caress you,
Who will cherish you,
For whom dost thou scatter this divine fragrance ?

Whose love is it that makes you so lovely?
Whose care keeps you,
Whose heart draws you
To don the radiant and glorious hue so comely?

What is it you whisper to the winds as they pass,
Swaying gently on your stem
Laughing, smiling at them,
You rejoice in their touch and gentle caress.

Do you not know that passion is ephemeral
He who you thrill to
With love who you long for,
The one who fills your heart with sweetness and delight,

Will after a day or two
He who you thrilled to
Joyously go seeking
For honey elsewhere.

Today he caresses you with ecstasy in his heart
Tomorrow when his rapture is broken
Your dream shattered with harsh words spoken
You will find him in the arms of another beloved.

Having deserted your love, he has forgotten all,
No tears will touch him,
No plea will reach him,
Tears futile from your soft heart will fall.

(Translated by Dr Sipra Mukherjee)

The Introduction to the Play *Apurba Sati* written by Sukumari Dutta (Golaapsundari)

PRO VIDEO[3]

Women Readers,

At a sudden glance even an ugly face when well-groomed charms the eye. Why does that happen? Is ornamentation the only reason for this? How many categories of appearances are there? We will now discuss only two. The first is an apparent beauty that attracts the eye and second, an enlightened spiritual beauty. Nothing that does not carry an inner light is beautiful. Then, my sisters, which light do you desire? You are educated and enlightened—which ornamentation do your highly educated minds desire?

The first level will satisfy the self and the second the universe. Are you then desirous of the first level? No. A highly educated mind can never lower the standard. Obviously the second is the target and it is the second level that the following piece hopes to identify with.

May the youthfulness in you and me through our youthful frivolity enchant the Bengalis with thoughts of the ideal of Bengal.

I present my first publication to the women of Bengal. My heart! Why do you feel such happiness in giving such a desired gift away? At last I realise why—If my sisters are not able to see their reflected images in the varied mirrors I portray then the incomparable expectations about the effect of mirrors that have arisen in my heart will be plunged into darkness now and for ever. But it is not appropriate that fear of disappointment should make me lose hope now. In this matter I expect neither your contempt nor your pleasure. I have achieved immeasurable happiness and inspiration through the pleasure of my presentation. If I am fortunate enough to receive your support, that would be beyond all my expectations.

Calcutta 3rd Sravan 1282 BS

Sri Ashutosh Das
Srimati Sukumari Dutta

NOTES

1. Dr Purna Chowdhury, Professor of English, Heritage College, Quebec, Canada.
2. Dr Sipra Mukherjee, Associate Professor of English, West Bengal State University, India.
3. This word has been translated by Amit Maitra in *Rangalaye Banganati* for the word *Agradrishta* used instead of the more conventional Bengali words for introduction. The rest of the translation is mine.

BIBLIOGRAPHY

Primary Sources

Bengali

Chowdhury, Ahindra, *Nijere Haraye Khunji*, vol. I, Calcutta: Indian Associated Publishing Company, 1962.

Dasi, Binodini, *Amar Kotha O Anyanyo Rachana*, ed. Saumitra Chattopadhyay and Nirmalya Charya, Calcutta: Subarnarekha, repr. 1987.

Dasi, Binodini, *My Story and My Life as an Actress*, ed. and tr. Rimli Bhattacharya, Delhi: Kali for Women, 1998.

Datta, Amarendra Nath, *Amara Granthabali,* 1902.

Datta, Michael Madhusudan, *Letters, Michael Rachanabali*, ed. Kshetra Gupta, Calcutta: Sahitya Samsad, 1984.

Devi, Nabin Kali, *Kamini Kalanka,* ed. Sumanta Banerjee, Calcutta: Wild Strawberries Books, 2010.

Dutt, Utpal, *Gadyasamagra*, vol. I, Collected Prose, ed. Samik Bandopadhyay, Calcutta: Dey's Publishing, 1998.

Ghosh, Girish Chandra, *Girish Rachanabali*, ed. Rathindra Nath Roy and Devipada Bhattacharya, Calcutta: Sahitya Samsad, 3rd edn., 1991.

Mukhopadhyay, Aparesh, *Rangalaye Trish Bochhor*, Calcutta: Granthan Publications, 1972.

Roy, Dwijendralal, *Dwijendra Rachabali,* ed. Rathindra Nath Roy, Calcutta: Sahitya Samsad, 3rd edn., vols. I and II, 1985.

Vidyasagar, Iswar Chandra, *Vidyasagar Granthabali*, ed. by Suniti Kumar Chattopadhyay, Brojendra Nath. Bandopadhyay and Sajanikanta Das, Calcutta: Vidyasagar Smriti Samrakshan Samiti: Ranjan Pub. House, 1938.

Vidyasagar, Ishwar Chandra, *The Selected Letters of Vidyasagar*, ed. by Santosh Kumar Adhikari, Calcutta: Vidyasagar Research Centre, 1985.

English

Pal, Bipin Chandra, *Memories of My Life and Times*, Calcutta: Bipin Chandra Pal Institute, 2nd revd. edn., 1973.

Secondary Sources

English

Bannerji, Himani, *The Mirror of Class: Essays in Bengali Theatre*, Calcutta: Papyrus, 1998.

Banerjee, Sumanta, *The Parlour and the Streets*, Calcutta: Seagull Books, 1989.

Banerjee, Utpal, ed., *Bengali Theatre 200 Years*, New Delhi, Publications Division:, Ministry of Broadcasting, Governement of India, 1999.

Benegal Som, *A Panorama of Theatre in India,* Delhi: Popular Prakashan, 1968.

Bennett, Susan, *Theatre Audiences*, London: Routledge, 1990.

Bhatia, Nandi, ed., *Modern Indian Theatre: A Reader*, New Delhi: Oxford University Press, 2009.

———, *Performing Women/Performing Womanhood: Theatre, Politics and Dissent in North Indian,* New Delhi: Oxford University Press, 2010.

Cameron, K.M. and Hoffman T.J.C., *The Theatrical Response*, London: Macmillan, 1969.

Chakraborty, Usha, *Condition of Bengali Women Around the Second Half of the Nineteenth Century*, Calcutta: Bardhan Press, 1963.

Chatterjee, Minoti, *Theatre Beyond the Threshold: Colonialism, Nationalism and the Bengali Stage 1905–1947*, New Delh: Indialog Publications, 2004.

Chatterjee, Sudipto, *The Colonial Stage: Theatre in Colonial Calcutta*, Oxford: Seagull Books, 2007.

Cima, Gay Gibson, *Performing Women: Female Characters, Male Playwrights and the Modern Stage*, New York: Cornell Univerity Press, 1993.

Dasgupta, Hemendranath, *The Indian Stage*, vol. III, New Delhi: Munshiram Manoharlal, 2002.

Dasgupta, M.K., *The Indian Stage,* vol. III, Calcutta: Girish Centenary Edition, 1944.

Dasgupta, Hemendranath, *The Indian Theatre*, vol. I, New Delhi: Gyan Publishing House, 1988, New edn. and repr., 2009.

Dharwadkar, Aparna Bhargava, *Theatres of India: Drama, Theory and Urban Performance in India since 1947*, New Delh: Oxford University Press, 2005.

Findlater, Richard, *The Player Queens*, London: Weidenfeld and Nicholson, 1976.

Guha, Thakurta Prabhu Charan, *The Bengali Drama: Its Origin and Development*, K. Paul, French, Trubner & Company, Limited, 1930.

Gupta, Charu, *Sexuality, Obscenity, Community: Women, Muslims and the Hindu Public in Colonial India*, The 'Opus 1' Series, New Delhi: Permanent Black, 2001.

Horrwitz, E.P., *The Indian Theatre: A Brief Survey of the Sanskrit Drama*, London: Blackie and Son Ltd., 1912.

Keith, A.B., *The Sanskrit Drama in Its Origin: Development, Theory and Practice*, Oxford:, Clarendon Press, 1924.

Lal, Ananda, ed., 'Oxford Theatres of India: A Concise Companion', New Delhi: Oxford University Press, 2009.

Levi, Sylvain, Le Theatre Indien, 1890, *The Indian Theatre*, tr. Narayan Mukherjee, Calcutta: Writers Workshop, 1978.

The Gospel of Sri Ramkrishna, tr. Swami Nikhilananda, Mylapore, Madras: Sri Ramkrishna Math, 1964.

Macqueen, Pope W., *Ladies First: The Story of Women's Conquest of the British Stage*, London, W.H. Allen, 1952.

Mukherjee, Sushil Kumar, *The Story of Calcutta Theatres 1753–1980*, Calcutta: K.P. Bagchi and Co., 1982.

Raha, Kironmoy, *Bengali Theatre*, New Delhi: National Book Trust, 3rd edn., 2001.

Rangacharya, Adya, *The Indian Theatre*, New Delhi: National Book Trust, 1971.

Ray Choudhury, Ranabir, *Calcutta: A Hundred Years Ago*, Bombay: Nachiketa Pub. Ltd., 1987.

Sampat, Vikram, '*My Name is Gauhar Jaan*': *Life and Times of a Musician*, New Delhi: Rupa & Co., 2010.

Sarkar, Sumit, *Writing Social History*, New Delhi: Oxford University Press, 1997.

Styan, J.L., *Drama, Stage and Audience*, London: Cambridge University Press, 1975.

Subramanyam, Lakshmi, ed., *Modern Indian Drama: Issues and Interpretations*, New Delhi: Srishti Publishers and Distributors, 2008.

Trussler, Simon, *Cambridge Illustrated History of the British Theatre*, Cambridge: Cambridge University Press, 1994.

Wilson, Horace W., *Select Specimens of the Theatre of the Hindus*, 3 vols., 3rd edn., New Delhi: Asian Education Services, 1984.

Bengali Books

Adhikari, Prabodhbandhu, *Natak O Rajneeti*, Calcutta: P. Sarkar, 1984.

Bagchi, Mani, 'Sisir Kumar O Bangla Theatre', Calcutta: Jignasa, 1960.

Bandopadhyay, Brojendra Nath, *Bangiya Natyashalar Itihas: 1795–1876*, Calcutta: Bangiya Sahitya Parishad Mandir, 1939, 6th edn., 1991.

Bandopadhyay, Sachindranath, *Natyadeuler Binodini*, Calcutta: Sahitya Vihar, 1987.

Banerjee, Sumanta, *Asruta Kanthaswar*, Calcutta: Subarnarekha, 2002.

Basu, Bishnu, *Babu Theatre*, Calcutta: Patibhas, 1986.

———, *Rajniti Natake Rajniti Theatre*, Calcutta: Delta Firma,1989.

———, *Theatre Bhabna*, Calcutta: Ganaman Prakashan, 1999.

———, *Rabindranather Theatre*, Calcutta: Pratibhas, 1987.

Bhattacharya, Ashutosh, *Bangla Natya Sahityer Itihas*, vol. I (1795–1872) and vol. II (1900–72), Calcutta: A. Mukherjee & Co. Pvt Ltd., 4th edn., 2003.

Bhattacharya, Manoranjan, *Theatre Prasange*, Calcutta: Pragati Lekhak O Shilpi Sangha 1st edn.

Bhattacharya, Sankar, *Natyacharya Sisir Kumar*, Calcutta: D.M. Library, 1976.

———, *Kolkatar Theatre*, vol. II, Calcutta: D.M. Library, 1972.

Bhattacharya, Upendranath, *Rabindra Natya Parikrama*, Calcutta: Orient Book Company, 1954, 6th revd. edn., 2008.

Chakraborty, Rathin, *Kolkatar Natyacharcha*, Calcutta: Pashchim Banga Natya Academy, Information and Broadcasting Department, Govt. of West Bengal, 1991.

Chakraborty, Rudra Prasad, *Rangamancha O Rabindranath: Samakalin Protikriya*, Calcutta: Ananda Pub. Pvt Ltd., 1995.

Chakraborty, Shambhu Nath, *Bingsho Shataker Theatre e Bangla Natok*, Calcutta: Kalyani Prakashani, 1994.

Chakraborty, Sudhir, *Dwijendralal Roy: Smaran Bismaran*, Calcutta: Pustak Bipani, 1989.

Chatterjee, Bijoy Krishna, *Bangla Natake Charitra Chitran*, Calcutta: Sarat Book House, 1987.

Chattopadhyay, Nalini Ranjan, *Sri Ramkrishna O Banga Rangamancha*, Calcutta: Mondal Book House, 1978.

Chowdhury, Ahindra, *Bangalir Natya Charcha* (Commemorating Centenary of Bengali Public Theatre), Calcutta: Shankar Prakashan, 1972.

———, *Bangla Natya Bibardhane Girish Chandra*, Calcutta: Bookland, 1959.

Chowdhury, Khaled, *Theatre e Shilpobhabna*, 3rd edn., Calcutta: Protikshon Pub. Pvt Ltd., 1997.

Das, Pulin, *Banga Ranga Mancha O Bangla Natok, Vol. I: 1795–1920*, Calcutta: M.C. Sarkar and Sons, 1983.

Datta, Ramapati, *Rangalaye Amarendranath*, ed. Debjit Bandopadhyay, Calcutta: Dey's Publishing, 2004.

Dutt, Utpal, *Chayer Dhoyan*, Calcutta: Rupa & Co., 1964.

Gangopadhyay, Abinash Chandra, *Girish Ghosh*, ed. Swapan Majumdar, Calcutta: Dey's Publishing, 2nd edn., 1993.

Ghosh, Ajit Kumar, *Natyatattva O Natyamancha*, Calcutta: Dey's Publishing 1991.

———, *Rangamanche Bangla Natoker Proyog*, Calcutta: Dey's Publishing, 1994.

———, *Bangla Natoker Itihas*, Calcutta: Dey's Publishing, 2005.

———, *Nataker Kotha,* Calcutta: Suprakash Pvt Ltd., 1959, Calcutta: Shaibya Pustakalay, 2nd edn., 1978.

———, *Natok O Natyakar*, Calcutta: Dey's Publishing, 2000.

Ghosh, Binoy, *Kolkata Shohorer Ittibritta: Town Kolkatar Korcha*, vol. II, Calcutta: Bak Sahitya, 3rd edn., 1997.

Guha, Aravinda, *Sajghar*, Calcutta: Tribeni Prakashan Pvt Ltd., 1961.

Gupta, Devnarayan, *Banglar Nat Nati*, 2 vols., Calcutta: Sahityalok, 1985.

———, *Nat Natider Bichitra Kahini*, Calcutta: Grantha Prakash, 1964.

———, *Shekaler Theatre O Beshbhusha*, Natyashodh Sansthan Bhashanmala 1, Calcutta: Thema, 2000.

———, *Natya Sanglaper Bibartan,* Calcutta: M.C. Sarkar & Sons, 1989.

———, *Nayika O Rangamancha,* Calcutta: Sacindranath Biswas, 1976.

———, *Wings er Arale,* Calcutta: M.C. Sarkar and Sons, 1978.

Gupta, Mahendranath, *Rangamancher Rup Trishna*, Calcutta: Sri Guru Library, 1368 BS (1961).

Gupta, Ramen, *Green Room Theke Court Room*, Calcutta: D.M. Library, 1970.

Maitra, Amit, *Rangalaye Banganati*, Calcutta: Ananda Pub. Pvt Ltd., 2004.

Majumdar, Debashis and Samaddar Sekhar, eds, *Shatabdir Natyachinta*, Calcutta: A. Mukherjee & Co. Pvt Ltd., 2000.

Mitra, Arun Kumar, *Amritalal Basur Jibani O Sahitya*, Calcutta: Navanna, 1970.

Mitra, Sambhu, *Kake bole Natyakala*, Calcutta: Ananda Publishers, 1st edn., 1991.

———, *Abhinoy Natok Mancha*, Calcutta: Satyabrata Library, 1957.

Mukhopadhyay Durgashankar, *Natya Tattva Bichar*, Calcutta: Modern Book Agency, 1984.

Mukhopadhyay, Kalish, *Bangla Natyashalar Itihash,* Calcutta: Star Theatre Pub, 1973.

Nandi, Saumendra Chandra, *Bangla Oitihashik Natok Samalochana*, Calcutta: Bangiya Natak Samsad Prakashan, 1981.

Patri, Purnendu, *Kolkatar Pratham*, Calcutta: Dey's Publishing, 2002.

Roy, Chowdhury Suvir, *Bilati Jatra Theke Swadeshi Theatre*, Calcutta: Jadavpur University, Comparative Literature Department, 1971.

Roy, Hemendra Kumar, *Bangla Rangalay O Sisir Kumar*, Calcutta: Orient Book Company, 1361 BS (1954).

———, *Shaukhin Natyalaye Rabindranath*, Calcutta: Indian Associated Pub Co., 959.

Sengupta, Pradyot, *Bangla Natok O Natyakar*, Calcutta: Sahitya Tirtha, 1969.

Sur, Atul, *She Ar Ek Kolkata*, Calcutta: Sahitya Lok, 1997.

Vidyabhushan Upendranath, *Ardhendushekhar*, Natya Pratibha Series, Kolkata: Sisir Publishing House, 1920.

———, *Tinkadi*, Natya Pratibha Series, 2nd Samkhya, Kolkata: Sisir Publishing House, 1919.

———, *Binodini O Tarasundari,* Natya Pratibha Series, 4th Samkhya, Kolkata: Sisir Publishing House, 1919.

Journals and Newspapers

English

Advance

Amrita Bazar Patrika

Bande Mataram

Bengal Times

Bengalee

Bombay Chronicle

Forward

Indian Mirror

Sangeet Natak

Bengali

Abhinaya
Bangla
Bangabasi
Mashik Basumati
Nachghar
Natyamandir
Natya Bharati
Rangamancha
Rangalaya
Saurabh
Sisir.

INDEX